Divine Tempest

Marie-Louise von Franz, Honorary Patron

**Studies in Jungian Psychology
by Jungian Analysts**

Daryl Sharp, General Editor

DIVINE TEMPEST
The Hurricane
As a Psychic Phenomenon

David E. Schoen

To all those people and their contributions without which this book would truly not exist. For your letters, articles, poems, stories, ideas, artwork, dreams and inspirations, I thank you, and especially my spouse, Peggy DesJardins; my good friend, Rita Breath; my typist, Peggy Brannan; my thesis supervisers, Jan Clanton Collins, John Desteian and Julia McAfee; the members of the C.G. Jung Society of New Orleans; and Lyn Hill Hayward.

Canadian Cataloguing in Publication Data

Schoen, David E. (David Edgar), 1951-
    Divine tempest: the hurricane as a psychic phenomenon

(Studies in Jungian psychology by Jungian analysts; 78)

Includes bibliographical references and index..

ISBN 0-919123-79-1

1. Hurricanes—Psychological aspects.
I. Title. II. Series.

QC941.8.S36 1998   551.55'2'019   C97-931885-8

INNER CITY BOOKS
Box 1271, Station Q, Toronto, Canada M4T 2P4
Telephone (416) 927-0355
FAX 416-924-1814

Honorary Patron: Marie-Louise von Franz.
Publisher and General Editor: Daryl Sharp.
Senior Editor: Victoria Cowan.

INNER CITY BOOKS was founded in 1980 to promote the understanding and practical application of the work of C.G. Jung.

Cover: The Big Eye. (Monique Salaber/Liaison International).

Printed and bound in Canada by University of Toronto Press

CONTENTS

5

See final page for descriptions of other Inner City Books

Illustrations and Credits

page 11. Eye of hurricane. Monique Salaber/Liaison International.
  12. Aftermath of Hurricane Andrew, Homestead, Florida, 1992. AP aerial photo, left half (see page 69 for right half).
  29. Hurricane warning flags and meteorological insignia. U.S. Weather Bureau.
  30. Rudra, Vedic god of storms. Ellora cave temple, 8th cent. A.D. *New Larousse Encyclopedia of Mythology*, p. 341.
  37. Typhon. Detail from a red-figured vase. *New Larousse Encyclopedia of Mythology*, p. 91.
  42. Adad, Babylonian god of tempests. Stele, Arslan-Tash, 8th cent. B.C. *New Larousse Encyclopedia of Mythology*, opp. p. 53.
  46. "Then the Lord answered Job out of the whirlwind." Engraving. William Blake, *Illustrations of the Book of Job*.
  53. Pre-Columbian Ciboney Indians' hurricane totem, compared to U.S. Weather Bureau hurricane insignia.
  69. Aftermath of Hurricane Andrew, Homestead, Florida, 1992. AP aerial photo, right half (see page 12 for left half).
  76. *To Shelter*. Ceramic scuplture by David Martinez, 1994. Photo by Rick Gardner, Houston.
  80. Processional cross bent by Hurricane Camille, August 17, 1969. Christ Episcopal Church, Bay St. Louis, Mississippi.
  89. Medusa's eye and Great Mother's eye. Marion Woodman, *Addiction to Perfection*, 1982, p. 32.
  90. Spiral mandala. Painted dream image. C.G. Jung, *Man and His Symbols*, p. 227.
  101. The uroboros as mystic wind heaving over the waters. Monoprint by Vicki Cowan, 1996.
  113. Cloud of Chaos. Marolles, *Tableaux du temple des Muses* (1665). British Museum.

Preface

I'm in a house with other people. The house is on pilings out over
the water from the shore. The wind is so strong it is rocking the
house, people are being thrown against the walls, waves and water
are everywhere. I can see the spray and water all around through the
windows. It is a hurricane. The house stays together and holds
against the storm. The waves are hitting the windows.
It is a Category One storm.

—Dream of a 16-year-old boy, September 1993.

The Wind of Pentecost

The Spirit lifts His inner crying,
and wind that on a ruined plain
sets a debris of echoes flying
does not so vehemently strain.

Whither, I ask, this rush of yearning
divinity? And dare I guess
that Love, the gale of God, is turning
towards acres of my nothingness?

Zephyr and gentle breeze they say You
and so You are in Your domain,
But if it please You, God, I pray You
possess me as a hurricane.

And name this as my consolation
who must be humbled since I sinned,
that death and loss and devastation
present no obstacle to wind.

O Love, the vast and unabated
make me Your wasteland, lone and lost,
divested earth alone created
to hold the Wind of Pentecost.

—Jessica Powers. [1]

---

[1] *Selected Poetry of Jessica Powers*, p. 26.

Lord how the ponds and rivers boiled
And how the shingles rattled
And oaks were scattered on the ground
As if the Titans battled.

And all above was in a howl
And all below a clatter—
The earth was like a frying pan
Or some such hissing matter.

—Oliver Wendell Holmes, 1841.[2]

The winds, running around the circle, howled and whistled,
and screeched like a thousand demons.

—Raphael Semmes, Captain of the Warship Alabama
during the Civil War, 1862.[3]

There are indications that physical energy and psychic energy may
be but two aspects of one and the same underlying reality. If this
turns out to be the case, then the world of matter will appear as, so to
speak, a mirror-image of the world of spirit or of the psyche,
and vice versa.

—Marie-Louise von Franz.[4]

The common background of microphysics and depth-psychology is
as much physical as psychic and therefore neither, but rather a third
thing, a neutral nature which can at most be grasped in hints
since in essence it is transcendental.

—C.G. Jung.[5]

---

[2] Marjory Stoneman Douglas, *Hurricane,* p. 209.
[3] Ibid., p. 228.
[4] *C.G. Jung: His Myth in Our Time,* p. 236.
[5] *Mysterium Coniunctionis,* CW 14, par. 768. [CW refers throughout to *The Collected Works of C.G. Jung]*

Introduction

I was born and raised in south Louisiana, never very far from the great Gulf of Mexico, hence hurricanes have always been a part of my life geographically and psychologically.

My earliest memory of a hurricane was in the 1950s when I was four or five years of age. I remember flood waters three feet high everywhere around my house in New Orleans. It was exciting and novel: cars parked on neutral grounds, boats floating by the front door, my whole neighborhood a giant swimming pool. Hurricane Betsy in 1965 touched me in a different way. I walked through National Guard tents with hundreds of homeless frightened families huddled together around Army cots, with only meager possessions hastily salvaged from the devastating storm. I saw the mark of floodwaters to the ceiling, almost engulfing the house of a classmate in Chalmette.

In 1969, I walked where the awesome power of Hurricane Camille had taken out complete highways in Bay St. Louis, Mississippi, and swept away whole buildings, leaving nothing but the foundations and concrete slabs. I played touch football once in the eye of a smaller storm during my college days in Lafayette, Louisiana. I've witnessed towering pine trees (with roots half a mile deep), sway and snap like twigs before the mighty hurricane. I've weathered Hurricanes Juan and Andrew and dozens of others through the years. I dream of hurricanes, too.

For me and for most people living along the Gulf Coast the hurricane has always been an integral part of our experience, our lore, our culture, our collective psyche. Hurricanes are mysterious, dangerous, fascinating, exciting, frightening, unpredictable, awesome, powerful, special, fun, deathly destructive and uncontrollable. They are interwoven in the fabric and texture of our way of life and our way of looking at life—Let the good times roll, for tomorrow may not come. They fall into a special category of our culture, like

9

Mardi Gras, jazz funerals and the rare snowstorm. We live with the hurricane and it lives within us. Hurricanes move us literally and figuratively, inwardly and outwardly. The hurricane season is paradoxically both feared and anticipated with edgy delight.

The experience of the hurricane is imprinted deeply in me, and its gale force winds have never ceased to whirl powerfully through my veins. This is why I was moved on a personal level to write about hurricanes; they are so close to my spirit and to my soul.

From my subjective experience, I then formulated objective, theoretical questions: What does the hurricane represent in the psyches of human beings? What does the image of the hurricane signify in human history, literature and myth? What does it mean in dreams, fantasies, imagination and actual experience? How does the image of the hurricane act upon the human psyche, and how does the human psyche act upon and modify the image of the hurricane for its own purposes? How can the hurricane be viewed psychologically, especially from a Jungian perspective?

It is to these overarching questions that this book is addressed. I am more concerned with the overview, the big picture of the hurricane, than with attempting to track down every possible allusion and detail associated with it.

My hypothesis is that the hurricane is a universal symbol reflecting an archetypal image of the Self in perhaps its most primordial form. It echoes deeply within the psyches of both aboriginal and modern peoples, whose attempts to deal with it, inwardly and outwardly, have both similarities and differences based on the assumptions and world views of each.

I will demonstrate this through exploration of the meteorological and historical facts about hurricanes, mythological and anthropological amplification, modern dream material and actual experiences. Finally, my conclusion will synthesize the preceding information into a cohesive, theoretical construct from the point of view of Jungian psychology.

The preface to this work includes four examples of the hurricane as a psychic phenomenon: as the central image in a dream, as the inspiration for a poem about being possessed by God, and as the profound actual experience of the hurricane moving two men to write of it. The quotes from Marie-Louise von Franz and Jung approach the liminal question of inner and outer reality, the world of matter versus the world of psyche: What comes first, the image or the hurricane?

Into the mystery of the eye, I proceed . . .

1
Meteorological and Historical Facts

Background: Power and Might

They are the greatest and most destructive storms on the face of the Earth. In the North Atlantic and Eastern North Pacific Oceans, they are known as hurricanes. In the Western Pacific, they are called typhoons. In the Indian Ocean, they are called cyclones.

Hurricanes kill more people each year than all other storms combined. Interestingly, they are not the biggest storms, nor do they produce the fastest winds. The giant mid-latitude storms that occur in the middle of the Atlantic and Pacific Oceans are the biggest. They can reach sizes of 1,800 miles across; they spin more slowly and over a much greater area than hurricanes, which measure 200-500 miles across. The mid-latitude storms can be over three times larger than the largest hurricane. The fastest winds on earth belong to the tornado, which can reach to over 300 mph. The strongest hurricanes in the Atlantic have recorded sustained winds up to 200 mph.[6] A Category Five hurricane, which is the worst kind, has sustained winds of 156 mph or higher. Typhoon winds in the Pacific Ocean can go over 250 mph, because the Pacific Ocean is wider than the Atlantic and storms have more time and area to increase in strength and size.

The power of a hurricane is truly awesome. How awesome? If the energy expended by an average hurricane in one day could be converted into electricity, it could supply the electrical needs of the entire United States of America for six months. The life span of an average hurricane is eight to twelve days. That would be enough power to light up the United States for four to six years—from just one hurricane—incredible! The life span of a hurricane can be as

---

[6] Clint Twist, *Repairing the Damage: Hurricanes and Storms*, p. 9.

brief as a few hours or as long as over a month.

Another example of the magnitude of the power of a hurricane is that the energy equivalent of one hurricane in one day would equal eighty earthquakes the size of the one that destroyed San Francisco in 1906 (8.3 on the Richter scale). For comparison purposes, the 1906 earthquake was more than ten times as powerful as the 1989 earthquake (6.9) which canceled the World Series game at Candlestick Park in San Francisco. This 1989 quake was even stronger than the more recent 1994 Los Angeles earthquake (6.6), which was devastating. Sometimes it is difficult even to try to imagine the power of a hurricane. The heat energy released by one hurricane in one day would equal the blast from the simultaneous explosion of 400 hydrogen bombs of a 20 megaton size.[7] Remember that one hydrogen bomb is hundreds of times more powerful than the atomic bomb that destroyed Hiroshima and Nagasaki in 1945.

Some people, impressed by the comparatively awesome power and gigantic mushroom cloud of the atomic bomb, suggested it might be dropped into the eye of a hurricane to break it up. However, as one commentator suggests, trying to stop a hurricane with an atomic bomb would be about as effective as trying to stop an elephant stampede with a B.B. gun.[8]

The deadliest hurricane (cyclone) in history hit the mouth of the Ganges River in November, 1970, slamming into the coast from the Indian Ocean. More than one million people were killed. The devastation was so terrible that the region rebelled against the government of Pakistan and established the independent nation of Bangladesh. This storm is often referred to as the Bangladesh Cyclone of 1970.[9] A farmer who survived the storm recalls the scene:

> About dawn, the water began to go down. I could see bodies, hundreds of them, floating out to sea. At about nine in the morning, the water finally went down. My farm looked like a desert. There was

---

[7] Gary Jennings, *The Killer Storms: Hurricanes, Typhoons and Tornadoes*, p. 59.
[8] Ibid., p. 181.
[9] Norman Barrett, *Hurricanes and Tornadoes*, p. 20.

nothing left, but my family was all right. Only my aunt had been washed away with most of the old people. They were not strong enough to hold onto the trees.[10]

The deadliest hurricane to hit the United States was the Galveston Hurricane of 1900, which killed over 7,200 people. The deadliest hurricane to hit Louisiana was the Cheniere Caminada storm of 1893. It killed an estimated 1,500 people, mostly women and children who were not strong enough to hold on against the powerful waves and were swept out to sea—their bodies never recovered.

Most people are killed in hurricanes by water, not wind. Nine out of ten victims drown in the storm surge and flooding from the rain and waves.[11] Most damage to buildings and property is first from the storm waves, second from the rain and third from the winds.[12]

The highest storm surge recorded was by Hurricane Camille in 1969. She flooded the Gulf Coast of Mississippi and killed more than 300 people in seven states. Her storm surge was measured at 25 feet.[13]

The costliest hurricane to hit the United States and the costliest natural disaster in American history to date is, without question, the terrible Hurricane Andrew of 1992. He caused over $30 billion in damage. Hurricane Hugo in 1989 was second in history with $7 billion. Camille was third in 1969 with $3.8 billion. Hurricane Betsy in 1965 was America's first billion-dollar hurricane. Some say Hurricane Diane was first in 1955.

The lowest barometric air pressure ever recorded of a hurricane in the Western Hemisphere was in 1935. This unnamed storm killed over 400 people. Hurricane Gilbert in 1988 was the most powerful storm ever recorded in the Western Hemisphere. Hurricane Beulah in 1967 holds the record for the most tornadoes spawned by a hurricane: 155.

---

[10] Jennings, *Killer Storms*, p. 20.

[11] Dennis Brindell Fradin, *Disaster! Hurricanes*, p. 48.

[12] Jennings, *Killer Storms*, p. 74.

[13] Barrett, *Hurricanes and Tornadoes*, p. 30.

It is interesting to note that the hurricane in one way or another contains and contributes to all other types of storms and natural disasters. Hurricanes incorporate torrential rains, thunder storms and lightning. They also involve tidal waves and gale force winds. They cause flooding and mud and land slides. Tornadoes are a primary spin-off phenomenon of hurricanes. There is even evidence that hurricanes contribute to blizzards, as excessive moisture moves north into colder regions and results in driving snowstorms. One such storm in 1966 traveled 15,000 miles and went farther north than any other hurricane known in history. It traveled through Norway, Sweden, Finland and Russia, and finally died somewhere near the North Pole.[14]

Some scientists believe a great earthquake in 1923 in Japan was partially caused and assisted by a typhoon that was applying a significant imbalance of pressure on the fault line, enough to trigger the earthquake.[15] The Great New England hurricane of 1938, which killed 600 people on Long Island, New York, registered shock waves on seismographs over 3,000 miles away.[16]

Hurricanes also contribute to volcanic eruptions as the driving rains seep down, deepening the cracks in the volcanoes, helping to create more eruptions. This is how most of the Caribbean Islands were created—through volcanic lava flow.

Hurricanes also contribute to disease and epidemics, as people are forced to deal with contaminated drinking water, spoiled food, untreated wounds, undisposed-of corpses of humans and animals, and untreated sewerage. People are also threatened and killed by snakes, alligators, rats, dogs and other animals, frightened and stranded, competing with humans for dry space above the flooding on roofs, hills and in trees. In the race for survival, sometimes the humans lose. There are even recorded cases of people dying from heart attacks brought on by a hurricane.

---

[14] Jennings, *Killer Storms,* p. 81.

[15] Ibid., p. 93.

[16] Ibid., p. 97.

Indeed, the hurricane deserves its billing as the greatest and deadliest storm on the planet.

Vital Statistics: Birth and Death

In the Northern Hemisphere, the hurricane season is from June to November, but an occasional out-of-season hurricane has come as early as January and as late as December. In the Southern Hemisphere, it is just the reverse—from November to June.

Hurricanes turn counterclockwise in the Northern Hemisphere and clockwise in the Southern. All low pressure air follows this principle because of the earth's rotation, known as the Coriolis force. This is also why water spirals in one direction or the other as it goes down the drain. Interestingly enough, tornadoes are known to spiral in either direction in both hemispheres.[17]

Hurricanes measure from 200 to 500 miles in diameter. The eye of an average hurricane is 14 to 25 miles across. In larger storms, the eye can be up to 50 miles wide. Hurricanes can climb to heights of over eight miles. They can stand still or move in any direction, at speeds up to 60 mph. The average life span of a hurricane is 8 to 12 days. They can live only a few hours or for over a month, as mentioned previously.[18]

Hurricanes, in contrast to tornadoes, develop exclusively over salt water oceans. The surface temperature of the ocean must be higher than 80 degrees Fahrenheit to give birth to a hurricane. They do not arise within 450 miles north or south of the equator, because the Coriolis force there is not strong enough to form the spiral eye of the storm.[19] Hurricanes do not occur at all in the South Atlantic Ocean because the waters are too cold.

It is impossible to explain exactly what causes a particular hurricane. Something makes a slight disturbance in the atmosphere, usually in the doldrums of the tropics. The conditions for the birth of a

---

[17] Walter Copes, interview, Oct. 5, 1993.

[18] Sally Lee, *Hurricanes*, p. 14.

[19] Twist, *Repairing the Damage,* p. 16.

storm are a cloudless, calm sky with the sun beating down on still ocean waters warmed to over 80 degrees Fahrenheit. The disturbance in this quiet, calm scene could be a butterfly flapping its wings in the jungle, someone clapping their hands, a seabird landing over the water or a thunderstorm that rises up in the mid- afternoon heat.[20] Whatever it is, it disturbs the air and creates an updraft. Warm air rises and surrounding air moves in to take its place, and in turn it, too, rises. Slowly, the updraft builds in strength and air is sucked in from an ever-increasing expanse of hundreds of miles of ocean. The air begins to spiral because of the Coriolis force. The spin increases and gradually the spiral forms a chimney which increases the efficiency of the updraft, extracting heat and spewing out used air at the top.[21]

Initially, the disturbance is called a tropical depression, which is defined as moving winds of less than 39 mph. As it strengthens, it becomes a tropical storm with winds over 39 mph. When its winds reach 74 mph or higher, it is upgraded to a hurricane. At this point, it is no longer just a number but is given a human name.

Estimates are that a million tons of warm air are sucked up by the eye of an average hurricane every second.[22]

The hurricane is a creation of the sea and the winds. It is the only form of storm that can change the normal progress of the tides, their flow or volume.[23]

So, as the tropical storm becomes a hurricane, it turns itself into a gigantic, self-contained, self-operating, self-perpetuating, heat energy engine. The warm moist air is its fuel. As long as it is given fuel, it can run, grow and strengthen indefinitely.

To humans, one of the most striking aspects of the hurricane is the sound it makes, its infamous, steady, howling roar, described by many as the strangest, most frightening noise they have ever heard.

---

[20] Ibid.

[21] Ibid., p. 17.

[22] Jennings, *Killer Storms,* p. 55.

[23] Douglas, *Hurricane,* p. 9.

A woman who lived through the direct hit of Hurricane Camille describes the experience of the sound as "like holding on for dear life underneath a huge locomotive train barreling down the tracks."[24] (Her house was literally swept away. Somehow, miraculously, she and all her family survived.) Another man says, "It sounded like a thousand freight trains and a thousand airplanes coming right at you. It was horrendous—enough to deafen you."[25] Some call it an "eerie ceaseless howling," a "banshee wail," "the scream of the devil." Some people who have heard the roar have actually died of heart attacks. Joseph Conrad, in his novel *Typhoon,* describes the nightmarish sounds as "howls and shrieks which seemed to take on something of human rage and pain."[26]

It is interesting to note how often the roar of the hurricane is described as a locomotive engine and how often in meteorological terms it is described as an enormous, self-perpetuating heat engine.

A hurricane starts from nothing—it literally forms out of the empty void, as in Genesis 1:1-2:

> In the beginning God created the heavens and the earth, the earth was waste and void; darkness covered the abyss and the spirit of God was stirring above the waters.[27]

The exact mechanism that initiates the creation of a hurricane is still a mystery, and may remain so forever. There is a new branch of mathematics and physics called dynamic chaos theory which examines principles of unpredictability. Some scientists believe that chaotic dynamics may provide a useful perspective on weather patterns and especially hurricanes.[28]

Even though it is not known exactly how hurricanes are conceived, we do know what kills them. Essentially, they starve to death once their supply of heat and moisture is cut off, once there is

---

[24] Rita Breath, interview, Nov. 14, 1993.

[25] Fradin, *Disaster!,* p. 26.

[26] *Typhoon,* pp. 281, 287.

[27] *Holy Bible: Saint Joseph Textbook Edition.*

[28] Twist, *Repairing the Damage,* p. 16.

no more fuel to keep the engine going. Land and cold are the deadly enemies of the hurricane. Once it leaves the sea, it is doomed to die sooner or later. Land not only cuts off the fuel supply, it also offers resistance to the storm, slowing it down and helping to break it up. At sea, if the hurricane moves far enough north or south, depending upon the hemisphere, into colder waters, it freezes to death.[29]

In an average year, the North Atlantic produces about 100 disturbances. About six of these mature into full blown hurricanes. Why the other 94 do not become hurricanes under basically the same weather conditions is not understood—another mystery to add to the many associated with hurricanes.

About 70 percent of North Atlantic hurricanes come from a place 300 miles off the coast of the African continent, near the Cape Verde Islands. These storms have 2,500 miles of warm, tropical ocean to cross and thereby grow in strength before they hit the Americas. It seems no accident that mysterious Africa, symbol of the primal, unconscious shadow of the West, should be, as one writer puts it, "the breeding ground of the most vicious . . . most ferocious and terrible of all hurricanes, the Cape Verde Storms."[30]

The heaviest wind and waves of the hurricane occur on the right-hand edge of the storm wheel. Meteorologists consider heavy rain to be more than three-tenths of an inch of rain per hour. Hurricanes can dump five times that amount, spilling over an inch and a half of rain per hour. In 24 hours, that can leave over three feet of water covering everything—just from rain. To this, add hurricane waves which can reach heights of 70 feet or more (higher than a five story building). The ground on which most of our coastal cities are built is lower than 70 feet. It is an incredible amount of water to consider at one time in one place.[31]

A newspaper article hypothesized what would happen if a Cate-

---

[29] Jennings, *Killer Storms,* p. 81.

[30] Douglas, *Hurricane,* p. 12.

[31] Jennings, *Killer Storms,* p. 75.

gory 4 or 5 hurricane came directly up the mouth of the Mississippi River from the Gulf of Mexico and hit New Orleans. It would be like a shotgun blast, literally drowning the entire city under 25 to 30 feet of standing water. The only dry areas would be buildings and land higher than 30 feet—a frightening scenario, as all of New Orleans is built on land below sea level.

Another very striking aspect of the hurricane is the eye of the storm. The lower the air pressure in the eye, the stronger the winds will be. The whole storm revolves around the eye as its center and source of power. It is a chimney of complete calm in the middle of some of the most violent, destructive energy there is, a paradox of stillness in the center of whirling wind and water. Remember that the eye can be up to 50 miles across. People have described being in the eye as "spooky," "strange," "eerie," "unreal" and "sacred." Perhaps Marjorie Stoneman Douglas sums it up best:

> Beyond the topmost vapors of the encircling clouds and winds there may be brilliant, blue sky with sun striking down to make the whiteness dazzling. It is a place of mysteries . . . men who have penetrated there in ships half wrecked . . . in airplanes . . . speak of this place with awe.[32]

This numinous quality of the eye is an aspect of the hurricane that will be amplified later in chapter four.[33]

In the past, inexperienced people were often fooled by being in the eye, thinking the storm had passed and was all over, only to be surprised and shocked when the other half hit. There is also a common misconception that the eye is always completely clear and blue, without clouds; in fact, these conditions only occur some of the time.

---

[32] *Hurricane,* p. 16.

[33] "Numinous, like numinosity, comes from Latin *numinosum,* referring to a dynamic agency or effect independent of the conscious will. Descriptive of persons, things or situations having a deep emotional resonance, psychologically associated with experiences of the Self." (Daryl Sharp, *Jung Lexicon: A Primer of Terms and Concepts,* p. 92)

Positive and Helpful Aspects

People do not often think about the beneficial aspects of hurricanes, but there are many to be considered. Of greatest significance is the fact that, without hurricanes, there would likely be no life at all on this planet. As humans, we are not accustomed to "thanking" the hurricane for our existence, but perhaps we should. None of us would be here today without the hurricane's creative contributions to the evolution of life itself.

The story begins three to four billion years ago. The entire atmosphere of the earth had cooled to a seething boil; an all-encompassing envelope of raging storms. Hurricanes dominated the planet. Over time, these storms interacted with inert elements and chemicals. Somehow, the elements and chemicals were energized by the great power of the storms, perhaps by the electricity of the lightning. Thus, complex organic compounds were created and this is believed to be the beginning of life. These compounds gradually evolved over millions of years into living organisms, which began their long evolutionary trek, eventually populating the planet with its vast variety of species, including human beings.[34] It is fascinating to imagine that the spiral, double helix structure of DNA, which is fundamental to the genetic coding of all of life, was originally imprinted, somehow, in some way, by the hurricane itself. How ironic, that back at the beginning of time, hurricanes were in fact not the great destroyers, but the great creators of life.

Another benefit of hurricanes is that they bring needed rain to many regions of the world:

> They douse forest fires, revive drought-stricken wetlands and stir up nutrients in coastal estuaries, the spawning grounds for commercial food fish. In tropical islands, hurricanes provide needed rainfall.[35]

They also are important to the world's heat transfer system. Hurricanes distribute and move tremendous amounts of heat and en-

---

[34] Jennings, *Killer Storms,* p. 49.
[35] *National Geographic,* Sept. 1980, p. 379.

ergy that build up in the tropics from the equator to cooler areas near the poles. This helps to maintain the equilibrium of temperatures around the world.[36]

Hurricanes are essential to the distribution of plant life, animals, fish and birds to new regions of the world. They can be carried for thousands of miles by the waves and the winds, and even in the eye itself, to distant places they have never been. Tropical seabirds have been found after hurricanes in Maine, New York, Vermont and Nova Scotia in Canada.[37]

Hurricanes can be helpful in unusual ways, too:

> In 1730, the once lush, green and flowery island of Martinque was being gnawed bald by a plague of red ants until a hurricane came along and drowned out the ant population.[38]

—thus saving the island from destruction.

Another story (with which New Orleanians might take issue) is that "in 1818 a hurricane sank four ships of the infamous, buccaneer pirate, John Lafitte," putting him into retirement from terrorizing the open seas.[39] Of course, in New Orleans Lafitte is viewed as a hero since he helped save the city from the British in the Battle of New Orleans in 1814.

The strangest story I have found is that of a fish processing plant on the coast in Cameron, Louisiana. Working at the plant was such a smelly, undesirable job that most of the men who worked there were former convicts. After Hurricane Audrey demolished the area in 1957, killing 550 people, not a single ex-con could be found, dead or alive. It is widely rumored that the chaos and confusion of the storm gave them the opportunity to relocate, change identities and start new lives. Certainly, for those who survived, the hurricane provided a unique kind of rebirth experience.[40]

---

[36] Lee, *Hurricanes*, p. 9.

[37] Douglas, *Hurricane*, p. 30.

[38] Jennings, *Killer Storms*, p. 111.

[39] Ibid., p. 90.

[40] Peter DesJardins, interview, Oct. 29 and 30, 1993.

History and Science

The awareness of hurricanes by human beings extends back before recorded history, as primitive peoples were confronted with the power, fury and destruction of these storms.

The first known written account of a hurricane comes from the ruthless Mayan, Bishop Landa, who burned the great Mayan documents and records. He wrote of a hurricane that severely damaged the city of Mayapan in 1464, referring to the storm as "a hurricane of four winds."[41]

Christopher Columbus saw a hurricane in the distance on his voyage to the Americas. Its winds helped him to cross the Atlantic. He returned to Spain from the West Indies island of Hispaniola using the word "hurricane" for the first time. He had heard the word used by the Mayans, referring to a mighty god, "Hurakan," who for them was synonymous with the great storms.[42]

In 1495, the first well-authenticated hurricane hit the colony of Cape Isabella, which Columbus had established just a few years earlier.[43] Thus, the word Hurakan (hurricane) entered the vocabulary and the consciousness of the European world. The hurricane was among the first, worst and most frequent dangers encountered by the Spanish explorers. So the name and the word stuck.

The hurricane is known by many other names. Filipinos know them as "baguios," the Japanese as "repus"; in Australia they are "willy-willies," in India "asifa-T." The Chinese refer to the hurricane as "ty-fung," meaning "great wind." European sailors found it easier to say "tuffoon" or "typhon," which they may have known from Greek mythology.[44] Thus, the word was corrupted and today we have the typhoon of the Western Pacific, along with the more general term, "cyclone," used in the Indian Ocean.

The English in the 1600s pronounced the word hurricane in vari-

---

[41] Douglas, *Hurricane,* p. 42.
[42] Ibid., pp. 45-49.
[43] Ibid., p. 51.
[44] Jennings, *Killer Storms,* pp. 20-21.

ous ways: "hurachana," "uracan," "herocano" (hero storm?), "hyr-racano" or "furicane" (fury plus hurricane?).[45] There is documentation as late as 1958 of names similar to hurricane still being used and spoken in the Caribbean by the half-Arawak, half-Carib tribes, meaning "evil spirit," names such as "Yuracan," "Yuruk," "Hyroro-kan," "Yurakon" and "Yoroko."[46]

Hurricanes on occasion have even changed the course of history. In 1588, the remnants of two Atlantic hurricanes were decisive in destroying the "Invincible Armada" of the Spanish Empire. The hurricanes combined with England's smaller but faster ships to sink the larger, slower Spanish fleet. If the Armada had been successful in defeating the English, North America would have been dominated from that time on by Spanish colonization, much like South America. And instead of the strong English and French influences on North American culture, we might all be speaking Spanish and enjoying siestas.[47]

Another interesting side light on the effect of hurricanes on history involves William Shakespeare, who was fascinated with the stories of hurricanes coming back from the English ships trading in the Caribbean and the colonies in Virginia. He wrote *The Tempest* on short notice for the festivities surrounding a royal marriage at the court of James I. The uninhabited island of *The Tempest* is believed to be Bermuda. He even refers to the familiar eerie, ceaseless roaring of the hurricane winds. In *King Lear,* he wrote, "Rage, blow you Cataracts and *Hyrricanos* spout."[48] It seems even the great Shakespeare was awed and inspired by the mystery of the hurricane. Indeed, one critic says, "Surely *The Tempest* is the loveliest thing ever to come out of a hurricane."[49]

Turning from history to science, the first scientific observations

---

[45] Douglas, *Hurricane,* p. 107.

[46] Ibid., p. 40.

[47] Jennings, *Killer Storms,* p. 27.

[48] Act 3, scene 2, lines 2-3.

[49] Douglas, *Hurricane,* p. 111.

of hurricanes probably began in the late 1800s by a man known as the "hurricane priest," Father Bento Vines, a Jesuit living in Cuba:

> He spent his life studying hurricanes. Using daily weather observations and reports from ships, he tracked the storms and predicted a hurricane hitting Cuba two days ahead of time in 1875.[50]

Father Vines's observations were the first systematic charting of hurricanes. Before that, there were spotty reports and stories from sightings or sinkings of ships at sea or once a hurricane hit land.

The U.S. Weather Service was established in 1870. Sigmund Freud was fourteen years old at the time. So, at approximately the same historical period, the emergence of a systematic scientific exploration of the inner environment (psychoanalysis) coincided with a systematic, scientific exploration of humanity's outer environment (U.S. Weather Service).

The next big step in hurricane observation came in World War Two during the 1940s, with the development of radar. For the first time, humans could see the outlines of a hurricane and the definition of the eye on a radar screen.

In 1943, Joseph Duckworth, a pilot in the U. S. Army, flew into and out of the eye of a hurricane two times in one day, the second time to prove to the weather officer that he had actually done it the first time. Thus were born the famous Hurricane Hunters, who became a regular meteorological tool for studying the size, growth, strength and direction of hurricanes by flying into the eye of the storm and recording indispensable first-hand information. In the Pacific Ocean, the Hurricane Hunters are known as the Navy's Typhoon Trackers.[51]

> In 1955, Americans watched for the first time on their television sets the approach of Hurricane Diane by use of a radarscope portrait of the oncoming storm projected onto the screens in their living rooms.[52]

---

[50] Lee, *Hurricanes*, p. 41.

[51] Ibid.

[52] Jennings, *Killer Storms*, p. 147.

Beginning in the 1960s with the launching of satellites around the earth, humans were able to see pictures of entire and complete storms from a vantage point high above the planet. This new instrument of meteorological observation was born as C. G. Jung died, in 1961, after a lifetime sketching the most complete picture of the human psyche available to date. Developments in meteorology and psychology seem to occur synchronistically.

The naming of individual hurricanes goes back to the Roman Catholic populations of Central America, where the people were accustomed to naming a storm after the saint on whose feast day the hurricane hit land. In Australia, hurricanes are sometimes named after unpopular politicians. The U.S. Weather Bureau at first designated storms by the letters of the alphabet. But from year to year this became confusing. Later, the Bureau used the "military alphabet"—Able for A, Baker for B, Charlie, Dog, Easy, Fox and so on. Young weathermen began to refer informally to the storms by the names of their girlfriends. This practice was formally institutionalized in 1953 when all hurricanes were named after women, the first being Barbara. One book about hurricanes even titles a chapter, "The Bad Girls of 1954," after the series of hurricanes that hit that year.[53] Interestingly enough, some people view the 1950s as the pinnacle of patronizing patriarchy.

If there was a particularly destructive storm, its name would be retired from the rotating list—a kind of infamous hall of fame for hurricanes. Honorees include the likes of Betsy 1965, Beulah 1967, Camille 1969 and Andrew 1992. In 1979, men's names were added, as well as Hawaiian and Spanish names. Bob was first in 1979.[54] It is interesting to speculate that the influence at that time of the women's movement extended even to the naming of hurricanes.

At the present time, three separate lists of names for each year

---

[53] Billye Walker Brown and Walter R. Brown, *Historical Catastrophes: Hurricanes and Tornadoes,* p. 61.
[54] Lee, *Hurricanes,* p. 20.

are kept for hurricanes: one in the North Atlantic, one in the Eastern Pacific, and one for typhoons in the Western Pacific. There is no tradition for naming cyclones in the Indian Ocean. The hurricane is unique in that it is the only type of natural disaster which human beings have anthropomorphized by giving it an individual human name. It is truly in a category of its own.

So the naming of hurricanes has moved from the saints, through the military, to projection onto women, and finally to gender and cultural equity.

Finally, two additional pieces of information related to hurricanes. The hurricane warning flags for ships consist of two square flags, flying one directly beneath the other. The flag is predominantly red with a black square center (opposite, figure one). One such flag is a storm warning of winds 55-73 mph. Two flags indicate a hurricane with winds of at least 74 mph. The obvious intention of the red flag is to be visible from the greatest distance and to clearly warn of dangerous weather. The doubling of the hurricane flag emphasizes and strengthens the significance and meaning of the sign, as well as its visibility, making it twice as important both literally and psychologically.

The meteorological symbol for a tropical storm is an empty circle with two extensions at the top and the bottom, protruding in a swirling wing-like fashion. The symbol for a hurricane is the same except the circle is completely filled in (figure two).

The next chapter will focus on mythological and anthropological information relevant to hurricanes and their meaning to humans.

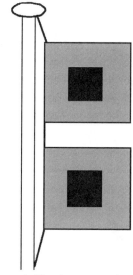

Figure 1. Hurricane warning flags.

Figure 2. Meteorological insignia for a tropical storm *(left)*
and for a hurricane *(right)*.

Rudra, Vedic god of storms

2
Mythological and Anthropological Perspectives

Introduction

To a great extent, mythological depictions of the hurricane follow the geography of the hurricane itself. Myths vary according to climate. The farther away people are from the actual experience of the hurricane, the more general is the image in their myth, if there is any at all. For example, Inuit, Nordic and North American Great Plains Indian myths have little or no imagery representing the hurricane directly.

As Joseph Campbell notes, "Geography shapes people's image of divinity. The god of the desert is not the god of the plains or the rain forest [or of the West Indies]."[55]

People who experience hurricanes themselves tell stories that are definite and detailed. Indian, Greek and Assyro-Babylonian myths paint a quite elaborate, descriptive picture of the hurricane.

Of course, the most specific imagery of the hurricane in the Western hemisphere comes from the people who know it the best, those who live in the West Indies, the Caribbean and Central America. Here the hurricane can be the most awesome and dominating theophany of their lives. It has divine status as the great, all-powerful, co-creator god, Hurakan, who touches every aspect of life and death.

Other factors besides geography condition the images inhabiting myth. Specific historical facts, such as rulers, wars, epidemics, emigrations, invasions, etc., as well as spiritual beliefs influence the shape of the myth. In some instances, cultures geographically close to the hurricane may have little mention of the hurricane in their myths due to the dominance of other influences. This seems to be

---

[55] Joseph Campbell and Bill Moyers, *The Power of Myth*, p. 101.

31

true in much of China, Japan and Oceania.

Various, more general aspects of hurricanes, such as wind, water, lightning, thunder, the storm and the whirlwind, are reflected in mythologies all over the world.

Ignorance, undiscovered cultures, unexplained archaeology, extinct oral traditions, as well as the bias of mythologists and this author, should all be kept in mind when considering the following mythological information on the hurricane.

Central American, Caribbean and West Indian Myths

Numerous tribes populated Central America and the islands of the Caribbean and the West Indies. The Mayans and the Aztecs dominated pre-Columbian culture with their profusion of divinities for everything imaginable. The myths of smaller tribal groups were often a mixture of local and Mayan and Aztec elements. Some form of the "Great Sun Myth," central to the Mayans and the Aztecs, can be found in almost all of these tribal mythologies. It is interesting to note that the sun is literally responsible for keeping the earth alive. It also causes all of the earth's weather by heating the air which creates winds, which become storms, which bring rain and can become hurricanes.

The myth of the hurricane is most alive here, where there are almost as many local versions, names and pronunciations as there are tribes. Most of the designations approximate the name Hurakan— which literally means "one-legged god."

In Guatemala and the West Indies, Hurakan ruled supreme. He was worshiped by all the other gods, including Gucamatz, the feathered snake, co-creator god of civilization and agriculture. Hurakan presides over and is the hurricane, the whirlwind and the rumblings of the thunderstorm. He is the great fertilizing creator-destroyer storm god. It is difficult at times to distinguish the god from the actual storm because in so many ways they are identical.

He gave the Quiche Mayans fire by rubbing his sandals together (perhaps a metaphor for lightning). His surname is Tohil, a name also given to Quetzalcoatl, the great sun god of the Aztec pantheon.

Guatemalan legend tells of the creation of the world:

> In the beginning, everything was under water, above which hovered
> Hurakan and Gucamatz, the givers of life. They said: "Earth!" and
> immediately the earth was created. The mountains rose out of the
> water, to the great joy of Gucamatz, who congratulated Hurakan. . . .
> The earth was covered with vegetation and the creators peopled it
> with animals with the command to do them homage.[56]

They then made clay and wooden men. The gods were unhappy
with these less-than-perfect creatures, so they destroyed them. Finally, they created four men out of yellow and white maize, then
they created four women, and these were the ancestors of the
Quiche Mayans. The parallels with the creation myth in Genesis are
striking, as is the actual part the hurricane has played in the creation
of the world.

Another version of the hurricane myth comes from the islands of
Cuba and Haiti where the Arawak tribes called their gods "Zemis."
There was a great goddess, Guabancex. She was the hurricane goddess, presiding over storms, winds and water. Her idol was made of
stone.[57] Legend has it that when villages displeased her, she became angry:

> [She] sent out her herald Guataba to order all the other gods to lend
> her their winds and their rains to be gathered up in the high valleys
> between the mountains and so to smash them down upon the vil-
> lages [probably flash flooding and mud slides on these islands].
> When the hurricane was upon them, the people shut themselves up
> in their leaky huts and shouted and banged drums and blew shell
> trumpets to keep the evil from destroying them.[58]

The stories of Hurakan and Guabancex, god and goddess, ruling
over the other gods, are both mythical versions of the hurricane itself, which stands above all other types of storms and for a time can
rule supreme over all nature.

The Mayan version of the destruction of the world, according to

---

[56] *New Larousse Encyclopedia of Mythology*, p. 439.

[57] Douglas, *Hurricane,* p. 39.

[58] Ibid.

an illustration covering the last page of the Dresden Codex, describes how the rain serpent will send "forth torrents of water. Great streams of water will gush from the sun and the moon."[59] Floods and cloudbursts will cause the symbolic universal destruction. Could it be that not only the creation of the world, as the Mayans knew it, but also its final destruction, would be caused by a ferocious, devastating hurricane? The hurricane would then take on the Self-like/Christ-like attributes of the Alpha and the Omega, the beginning and the end.

Indian Myth

Indian myth has several divinities whose qualities reflect central aspects of the hurricane. The god Varuna's stomach is made up of the two oceans of air and earth. He rules over the physical world, as well as the moral world. He controls celestial movements and the circulation of the waters; his breath is the wind.[60]

Siva, third person of the Hindu trinity, is the great destroyer and regenerator. He is addressed as the "god of gods" (the hurricane is the storm of storms). He carries a trident, like Poseidon and the devil. Like the eye of the hurricane, Siva sits in eternal meditation, the motionless center of movement. Siva's third eye and his philosophy is destructive of all illusion, much like the effects of the hurricane, which can strip humans materially, psychologically and spiritually down to the barest essentials. He determines the rhythm of the worlds, perpetual destruction and renewal, like the hurricane's dual aspect as giver and taker of life, moderator of heat and rainfall on the earth.[61]

Indra reflects many attributes of the hurricane in Indian myth. He is the warrior storm god like Wotan. He lives on Mount Meru, the center of the world. He is the lord of heaven and possesses the thunderbolt like Zeus and Adad from Babylonian myth. His essence combines cosmic energy and heroic strength. He is both the fertility

---

[59] Joseph Campbell, *The Hero With a Thousand Faces*, pp. 374f.

[60] *Larousse World Mythology*, p. 233.

[61] Ibid., p. 120.

and destroyer god. Like the hurricane, he sends floods, as well as rain, for the crops. Indra is the leader and king of all the gods. All the other gods enter into him, just as the hurricane is the container and king of all other storms. Indra is the only Vedic god who appears in human form, just as the hurricane is the only storm anthropomorphized with human names. He can also change shape like Poseidon and Proteus.

Indra has helpers in his work. Maruta, like Aeolus from Greek myth, is keeper of the winds and often accompanies Indra. Tvashtar forged the thunderbolt for Indra, similar to the original Cyclopes, who gave Zeus the thunderbolt and Poseidon the trident, which are both used to excite, execute and stir things up. Nothing stirs things up more than the hurricane. Tvashtar is the universal exciter in all forms; he is the equivalent of solar nature—heating things up, just as the elementary factors of heat and wind and water must be heated, moved and stirred up for the birth and epiphany of a hurricane.[62] There are many similarities with these images and the alchemical process of transformation, especially the interactions of *calcinatio* (heat), *solutio* (water) and *sublimatio* (air).[63]

Greek and Egyptian Myths

Trying to track down the hurricane in Greek myth is a fascinating and complicated endeavor. In some ways it is everywhere on the radar screen and yet it is difficult to quite put your finger on it as it keeps shifting into new and different forms. Each generation of the Greek gods and goddesses put its own spin on the sea storm and succeeding generations always incorporate, add or subtract from earlier versions. It can be confusing, but if we hold onto Ariadne's thread, we just might find our way through and catch a glimpse of Proteus in his hurricane form.

In the beginning was Oceanus:

---

[62] *New Larousse Encyclopedia of Mythology*, p. 326.
[63] See Edward F. Edinger, *Anatomy of the Psyche: Alchemical Symbolism in Psychotherapy,* chapters 2, 3, 5.

Some say that all gods and living creatures originated in the stream of Oceanus which girdles the world [like the uroboros]. He was one of those elemental forces [like the hurricane] which contributed to the formation of the world.[64]

Homer salutes Oceanus as "the essence of all things, even of the gods, and regards him as a divinity whose power was inferior to none but Zeus."[65] Oceanus was a Titan who originally ruled the sea. Tethys was his wife and bore him more than 6,000 children, including the water nymphs, all the waves on the seas of the world and all the river gods.

Hera and Amphitrite were the daughters of Oceanus and Tethys in some stories and were raised by them in others. Hera married Zeus/Jupiter and Amphitrite married Poseidon/Neptune. Oceanus thus continued to exert a significant influence on Olympus after his demise through the wives of the two most powerful male gods.[66]

Hera was originally a Great Goddess, Queen of Heaven, and worship of her preceded even that of Zeus. All the other gods rose in homage when she entered the assembly. Rage is associated with Hera's jealousy, as well as with the hurricane. Some interpret the noisy quarrels between Hera and Zeus as storms.[67] The winds were originally the property of Hera and the male gods had no power over them.[68] She was the patroness of Aeolus, keeper of the winds, and championed him among the gods. Hera also had power over sea storms, probably because of her original connection with Oceanus. She raised one such storm against Hercules that threw him onto the shores of the island Cos.[69] Poseidon never took kindly to anyone encroaching upon his sea-domain, including Hera. But she was the equal of Poseidon, and they usually fought to a draw.

Finally, and perhaps most significantly, Hera gave birth by her-

---

[64] Robert Graves, *The Greek Myths,* vol. 1, p. 30.

[65] *New Larousse Encyclopedia of Mythology*, p. 91.

[66] *Larousse World Mythology*, p. 119.

[67] *New Larousse Encyclopedia of Mythology*, p. 106.

[68] Graves, *Greek Myths,* vol. 1, p. 162.

[69] *New Larousse Encyclopedia of Mythology*, p. 173.

self to the most terrible monster of all, Typhon (below), because of her fury with Zeus for birthing Athene from his own body. Hera had a powerful, dark and destructive side. Besides creating Typhon, she nourished the Lernaean Hydra, sent serpents to kill Hercules as a baby, and struck many with madness. One way of looking at the hurricane is as the most monstrous, maddening, deadly, destructive storm created by the Great Goddess, Mother Nature (Hera).

Typhon, in other legends, is believed to be one of the sons of Aeolus, the wind god. Some stories place Aeolus as the son of Poseidon. This would then make Typhon Poseidon's grandson. Typhon is described by Isaac Asimov as "the largest monster who ever existed, hundreds of miles high and wide, his arms and legs ending in serpents."[70] He stirred up the winds, tossed the ocean and created terrible storms. He was called "the scourge of mankind."

---

[70] *Words from the Myths,* p. 110.

He is associated by the Greeks with Set, the god of absolute evil in Egyptian mythology and with Typhoeus, the monster, son of Tartarus and Gaea, who was created to battle with Zeus.[71]

In Egypt, the whirlwind is associated with Set/Typhon. Esther Harding says that Set/Typhon "is Eros in its unredeemed form, the under side, the opposite of relatedness."[72] Jung describes Typhon as that part of the soul which is "passionate, impulsive, irrational and truculent."[73] The hurricane, like Typhon, can be viewed as great, unredeemed energy potential, literally and psychologically, which winds up in impersonal, destructive contact with humans.

Typhon was the father of many monsters who personified the storm winds, which "pouncing suddenly on the darkened waves unleashed raging tempests to destroy men."[74] Typhon means "stupefying smoke." The Typhon sirocco in the desert brings bad dreams, murderous inclinations and rapes.[75] One author says, "Typhon *is* the spirit of the hurricane."[76] Socrates calls him "the personification of nature's destructive power."[77] Asimov believes that the word "Typhon" was picked up by the Arabs of the Middle Ages (from the Greeks, Romans and Egyptians), who then carried it to Southeast Asia where it is now used in the form of "typhoon," being synonymous with the word hurricane.[78] As mentioned previously, the Chinese word for hurricane is "ty-fung," meaning "great wind," and the similar phonetics of these two words probably contributed to their amalgamation, linguistically and mythologically.

Aeolus, as the wind god, like the hurricane, had the ability to use the winds for helpful or hurtful purposes. "If a storm were needed, he would plunge his spear into the cliffside of his walled island

---

71 Thomas Bulfinch, *Bulfinch's Mythology*, p. 952.
72 M. Esther Harding, *Woman's Mysteries: Ancient and Modern*, p. 196.
73 *Aion,* CW 9ii, par. 187.
74 *New Larousse Encyclopedia of Mythology*, p. 146.
75 Graves, *Greek Myths,* vol. 1, p. 135.
76 *New Larousse Encyclopedia of Mythology*, p. 146.
77 James Hillman and William Heinrich Roscher, *Pan and the Nightmare*, p. lxii.
78 Asimov, *Words from the Myths,* p. 111.

confining the winds, the winds would stream out of the hole it made, until he stopped it again."[79] He usually acted at the request of the other gods.

Poseidon, as the Greek god of the sea, ruled over all water, including lakes and rivers. He also claimed the air above the sea as his own and begrudged anyone else the right to raise storms over it. He considered Aeolus an illegal intruder. Poseidon was originally an ancient Pelasgian deity, older than Zeus. He was also the god of earthquakes. Because of his watery aspect, he was considered a god of fecundity and vegetation. The Spartans referred to him as Genethlios, "the creator." He is said to have been raised by Capheirra, daughter of Oceanus, and he married Amphitrite. In a sense, even the earth belonged to him, since it was sustained by his waters and he could shake it at will with his trident—capacities also belonging to the hurricane itself. Poseidon's appearance was usually accompanied by wild tempests, tokens of the god's furious rage.[80] When he and Hera battled, it must have been a sight to see.

No one ever disputes Poseidon's (or the hurricane's) rule over the sea, though he constantly challenged other gods over possession of different island territories. He usually lost on land, but would get his revenge by sending storms, floods, monsters and plagues, much like the hurricane, which ultimately loses to the land, but often at a great and long-remembered price. Poseidon's power was unshakable. He was known to send sea monsters to spray salt water (as the hurricane does) on crops to destroy them. Some versions say that, whenever Poseidon appeared on the ocean, there was a dead calm, like the eerie "calm before the storm," the often-noted stillness before the coming of the hurricane.[81]

Erich Neumann, interestingly, sees Poseidon, the consummate phallic-chthonic sea god, as belonging "by nature to the domain of the Great Mother, and not to that of the Great and Terrible Father,"

---

[79] *Bulfinch's Mythology,* p. 879.

[80] *New Larousse Encyclopedia of Mythology*, p. 133.

[81] Graves, *Greek Myths,* vol. 1, p. 59.

adding that "although Poseidon appears as an independent god, he remains the instrument of the Great Mother's destructive will."[82]

By analogy, it is true that the hurricane, like Poseidon, is from and of the sea, which has always been traditionally viewed as feminine—an image of the vastness and depths of the life-giving and taking aspects of the unconscious of humans and of the Great Mother mythologically. Neumann's comments, though, raise the question of whether projecting the terrible, destructive aspects of Poseidon (and of the hurricane) onto the feminine is correct archetypally or another example of the patriarchal bias that is certainly a part of the socio-political human history of the hurricane.

I have found numerous myths making a case for the hurricane as masculine and/or feminine in nature. As we shall see in chapter four, the hurricane is best viewed as an androgynous combination of god and goddess, since it seems to incorporate so much of both.

There are a number of lesser figures in Greek myth who should be mentioned as reflecting at least partial aspects of the hurricane. The original Cyclopes, not the one from Homer's Odyssey, were the three storm genii representing lightning, thunder and storm clouds. The Harpies were sea demons, tempest goddesses known as "the ravagers." The Chimaera was a hideous, monstrous personification of the storm cloud. Both the Harpies and the Chimaera were daughters of Typhon.[83] Zephyrus was the West Wind and Boreas the North Wind; both had histories as "savage and baleful winds."[84] Phorcys, the old man, ruled the waves and personified the evil sea. Triton, another son of Poseidon, "could raise and quieten the waves. . . . He personifies the roar of the sea with his blowing on the conch shell."[85]

More mention should be made of Set/Typhon from Egyptian myth. Set is the unruly, untamable one. He is the spirit of evil, al-

---

[82] *The Origins and History of Consciousness*, p. 178.
[83] *New Larousse Encyclopedia of Mythology*, p. 146.
[84] Ibid., p. 144.
[85] Ibid., p. 147.

ways in eternal opposition to the spirit of good. All that is destruction and perversity is from Set. He is often associated with the devil of Judeo-Christian tradition. He is the god of lust and desirousness, of unbridled instinct.[86] At times, human projections onto the hurricane are of an all-powerful, evil force echoing aspects of Set.

Assyro-Babylonian Myth

Originally in Assyro-Babylonian myth, Enlil, Lord of the air and the winds, was the god of the storm and the tempest. His weapon was the Amuru, that is, the deluge. He symbolized the forces of nature and was, like Varuna from Indian myth, considered the master of men's fates. He was the dispenser of good and evil and, like Yahweh, sent the flood in anger to destroy the human race.

After Enlil came Adad in the beginning of the second millennium B.C., god of lightning and tempest. "It is he who lets loose the storm, makes the thunder growl and bends the trees under the fury of the winds."[87] He is usually represented, as in the figure on the next page, standing on a bull and grasping thunderbolts in each hand. He also brought beneficent wind with its welcome rains to nourish the land, and thus was also (like so many others) considered a fertility god. Adad's job was to execute the will of Enlil.

Later, when the people of Babylon took over the gods of Sumer, Enlil became incorporated into the great hero god, Lord Marduk, who defeated Tiamat according to the ancient Babylonian Creation Epic. Tiamat is the Primordial Mother, personification of the sea and the blind forces of primitive chaos.

> She set up lizards, dragons, and sphinxes
> Hurricanes, mad dogs, scorpion-men,
> Lion-demons, fish-men, and centaurs,
> Bearing weapons that spare not, fearless in battle.
> Mighty are Tiamat's commands, irresistible are they.[88]

---

[86] Ibid., p. 19.

[87] Ibid., p. 60.

[88] From the Bablylonian Creation Epic, quoted by Jung in *Symbols of Transformation,* CW 5, par. 375.

In the great battle with Tiamat, Marduk forges his invincible weapons:

> He created the evil wind, Imhullu, the sou'wester, the hurricane,
> The fourfold wind, the sevenfold wind, the whirlwind and the
>   harmful wind.
>
> . . . .
>
> Then the Lord raised up the cyclone, his mighty weapon;
> For his chariot he mounted the storm wind, matchless
>   and terrible.[89]

After Marduk defeated Tiamat, "He cut up her bowels and made mincemeat of her heart, . . . / threw down her carcass and trampled upon it."[90] Then he created the world from her dismembered body.

It is significant to note in this myth that the storm winds of the hurricane not only precede, but are a necessary element in, the destructive act that leads to the creation of the world—once again echoing the original, essentially creative qualities of the hurricane.

Teutonic/Germanic Myth

Wotan/Woden/Odin is not only the principal god of the Teutonic peoples, but also of their hurricane. Wotan was originally the god of nocturnal storms. Hurricane lore holds that the storm strikes land most often in the dark of night. Like so many other storm gods, Wotan decides human fate. Wotan is the hunter—war god, god of fury and frenzy. He is "the sign of all the brute forces of the world, as distinct from its organized forces. He commands the physical world."[91] Nothing can stop him (or the hurricane) on his wild, impassioned hunts across the earth. He rules through magic and could change shape like Poseidon, Siva, Zeus and Proteus. Related to this magic is ESP/synchronistic phenomena associated with the hurricane (which will be addressed in the next chapter).

Jung says of Wotan that he can be spoken of as an archetype,

---

[89] Ibid., par. 376.

[90] Ibid., par. 377.

[91] *New Larousse Encyclopedia of Mythology*, pp. 253f.

rouser of tempests, unleasher of passions and lust. In reference to the rise of Nazism, he says:

> A god has taken possession of the Germans and their house is filled with a "mighty rushing wind." It was soon after Hitler seized power, if I am not mistaken, that a cartoon appeared in [the English magazine] *Punch* of a raving berserker tearing himself free from his bonds. A *hurricane* has broken loose in Germany while we still believe it is fine weather.[92]

> They [the Germans] are sucked like dry leaves into the roaring whirlwind.[93]

Wotan "seizes everything in [his] path and overthrows everything that is not firmly rooted."[94] He bows to no other god.

> [Wotan] represents a totality on a very primitive [unconscious, instinctual] level, a psychological condition in which man's will was almost identical with the god's and entirely at his mercy.[95]

Jung associates Wotan with Dionysus, Christ, the devil, the tribal god Yahweh, the Holy Spirit and Hermes, and says Wotan was considered identical to Mercurius by the Germans. Wotan also personified aspects of civilization. He was the god of science, wisdom and poetry. The hurricane too is linked in modern times with our unending scientific curiosity, a primevil kind of wisdom, and has been the inspiration for numerous poems and works of art. Thus does Wotan clearly reflect aspects of the hurricane.

In Teutonic-German myth, giants often personified natural phenomena such as volcanoes, earthquakes, hurricanes and winter. One giant, Aegir, was lord of the sea. His wife, Ran "the ravisher," stirred up the waves to destroy ships and capture men. She inspired terror and was so feared she was elevated to a veritable goddess.[96]

---

[92] "Wotan," *Civilization in Transition,* CW 10, par. 389 (emphasis added).
[93] Ibid., par. 398.
[94] Ibid., par. 391.
[95] Ibid., par. 394.
[96] *New Larousse Encyclopedia of Mythology,* p. 280.

Judeo-Christian Myth

Joseph Campbell refers to Yahweh as a storm-god. Yahweh in the Old Testament sends the sea storm to get Jonah (1:4),[97] speaks to the prophet Ezekiel (1:4) out of a storm wind,[98] and answers Job (38:1) out of the swirling whirlwind. An image of Job's experience appears in William Blake's series of engravings, *Illustrations of the Book of Job* (next page).

Yahweh is the universal creator-sustainer god. He is a mixture of opposites, loving and wrathful, creative and destructive, persecutor and helper (like the hurricane). Jung calls Yahweh "a moral antinomy"[99]—a totality of inner opposites—the indispensable condition for his tremendous dynamism, his omniscience and omnipotence. Elsewhere Jung says, "The forces of nature are always two-faced,"[100] having beneficent as well as destroying power, always ambivalent—and such is the case with Yahweh and the hurricane.

In Christian legend, Jesus demonstrates his power over the wind and the water when he orders the storm on the lake to calm and it miraculously obeys (Matt. 8:23-27):

> And when he was entered into a ship, his disciples followed him.
> And, behold, there arose a great tempest in the sea, insomuch that the ship was covered with the waves: but he was asleep.
> And his disciples came to *him,* and awoke him, saying, Lord, save us: we perish.
> And he saith unto them, Why are ye fearful, O ye of little faith? Then he arose, and rebuked the winds and the sea; and there was a great calm.
> But the men marveled, saying, What manner of man is this, that even the winds and the sea obey him![101]

---

[97] "But the Lord sent out a great wind into the sea, and there was a mighty tempest in the sea, so that the ship was like to be broken." (Authorized Version)

[98] "And I looked, and, behold, a whirlwind came out of the north, a great cloud, and a fire infolding itself, and a brightness *was* about it." (Authorized Version)

[99] "Letter to Père Lachat," *The Symbolic Life,* CW 18, par. 1555.

[100] *Symbols of Transformation,* CW 5, par. 165.

[101] Authorized Version.

Who is this that darkeneth counsel by words without knowledge

Then the Lord answered Job out of the Whirlwind

Who maketh the Clouds his Chariot & walketh on the Wings of the Wind

the Drops of the Dew

Hath the Rain

a Father & who hath begotten

WBlake invent & sculp

London Published as the Act directs March 8:1825 by William Blake N 3 Fountain Court Strand

Prou

The Holy Spirit descends on Pentecost in the form of a roaring, violent wind (Acts 2:1-3):

> And when the day of Pentecost was fully come, they were all with one accord in one place.
> And suddenly there came a sound from heaven as of a rushing mighty wind, and it filled all the house where they were sitting.
> And there appeared unto them cloven tongues like as of fire, and it sat upon each of them.[102]

Chinese, Japanese and Tibetan Myths

In Chinese myth, the Taoist religion recognizes only one god of thunder called Leikung, "My Lord of Thunder." He is an ugly, repulsive man with a blue body, wings and claws. He carries drums and holds a mallet and chisel, which he uses to create thunder and violent storms. Lightning is produced by Tien Mu, "Mother Lighting," rain by Yu-Tzu, "Master of the Rain." Clouds come from Yun-T'ung, "Little Boy," and the winds are produced by Feng-po, "Earl of Wind," an old woman who sometimes rides through the clouds on a tiger.

Four Dragon-Kings rule over each of the four seas. Their job is to distribute rain. Many people believe the dragons create storms, cause floods, landslides and earthquakes.[103]

The Chinese also have the principles of yin and yang, on which is based the I Ching. Yang is the masculine father principle representing the wind and the storm, thunder and lightning, the creative (Ch'ien, Hexagram 1). Yin is the feminine, mother principal representing water, the vast ocean, eternal being, the moisture of life, the receptive (K'un, Hexagram 2). The hurricane, like the yin-yang polarity, incorporates both principles into a oneness. Jungian analyst Marion Woodman says, "The differentiated ego, whether male or female, [cuts] a course between wind and water."[104]

In Tibet, there is a Buddhist tradition similar to the yin-yang

---

[102] Ibid.

[103] Jolande Jacobi, *Complex/Archetype/Symbol,* p. 148.

[104] *Addiction to Perfection: The Still Unravished Bride,* p. 15.

called yab-yum. Yab is masculine, father, eternity. Yum is feminine, mother, time. Together they form the oneness of the temporal and the eternal, and like the hurricane exist only for a short time, yet seemingly forever.[105]

The Japanese have a whirlwind god, Haya-ji, who releases the wind, as in many other myths, from a great bag. Like the Chinese, they have many separate gods of rain, wind, earthquakes, etc.[106]

In Tibet and Japan, the king was believed to rule the water and the rains. The weather depended on his will.[107]

Other Myths

Ancient myth holds that the Moon Goddess is the mother of all living things; not only is she the life giver, but also the destroyer.

> She creates all life on the earth and then comes the flood which overwhelms it. And this flood is her doing for she is [like the hurricane] the cause of rain and storm and tide and also of the flood. . . . [She] was thus giver of life and of all that promotes fertility, and at the same time wielder of the destructive powers of nature.[108]

In Slavic myth, the hurricane is created by

> the Tsar of the Sea who danced so furiously that he caused a tempest and innocent sailors perished. In order to stop the dancing and the attendant hurricane—the strings of the gusli [a musical instrument] were broken.[109]

The Hopi Indians of the Southwest have numerous spirits called Kachinas. The Kachina Sotukangu, "Heart of the Sky God," controls dangerous thunderheads, lightning and destructive rain. He is also an indomitable warrior, just like Wotan and Indra.[110]

In Africa, weather kings are common. They control wind, storms

---

[105] Campbell, *The Hero with a Thousand Faces*, p. 170.

[106] *New Larousse Encyclopedia of Mythology*, p. 416.

[107] James G. Frazer, *The Golden Bough: The Roots of Religion and Folklore*, p. 44.

[108] Harding, *Woman's Mysteries*, pp. 109ff.

[109] *New Larousse Encyclopedia of Mythology*, p. 298.

[110] Barton Wright, *Hopi Kachinas*, pp. 62ff.

and rain, both good and bad. They would either be deprecated or implored.[111]

Anthropological Aspects

Humans have from the beginning of their first contact with hurricanes tried to divert or control them. In the West Indies, when Hurakan and Guabancex were rampaging through the islands, the natives huddled in their huts, shouted, beat drums, shook rattles and blew shell trumpets in the hope that the noise would scare the gods away. When the Spanish colonists came to the islands, they tried to ward off the hurricane, which was now believed to be the devil's domain, by having the local priest parade the crucifix and other holy objects through the streets.

A Mass formulary entitled *Ad Tempestates Repellendas,* "For Averting Storms," composed by the Vatican, predating the first edition of the Roman Missal in 1474 and included ever since, was prayed urgently at these most frightening of times. The text almost seems to have been written specifically for the hurricane:

> We beseech Thee, O Lord, that all wickedness being driven away from Thy house, the fury of the raging tempest may pass away.[112]

Today in Louisiana in the Roman Catholic liturgy of the Mass, petitions are still made during the "Prayers of the Faithful," asking God, Our Father, through the intercession of Our Lady of Prompt Succor (who in New Orleans history saved the city several times from destruction by epidemics, fire and the British), to "spare us from all harm during this hurricane season and protect us and our homes from all disasters of nature."

Ancient or modern prayer has always been a very human response to the overwhelming dangers of the hurricane. In addition to prayer, every house and ship in the islands hung up a "cord of St. Francis," a rope tied into three knots of three turns apiece, whose

[111] Frazer, *The Golden Bough,* p. 44.

[112] *Saint Andrew Daily Missal;* thanks to Abbott Patrick Reggan, OSB, St. Joseph Abbey.

function was to "bind the winds."[113] It was believed the knotted cord around the saint's waist drove away the devils of the storm.

In the West Indies, the month of October, the worst for hurricanes, was dedicated to St. Francis of Assisi. A whole body of legends and lore grew up around petitions to the beloved saint, whose brotherliness encompassed all of nature. He was referred to as "Saint Francis of the Hurricane," and in the "Congo cult" he became a lesser deity of great power.[114]

It is interesting to note by extension how the winds play such a magical role with so many peoples. Breton peasants believed there was a devil in a gust of wind. German peasants believed there was a witch or a wizard in a whirlwind.[115] Witches in England, Scotland and Brittany, carrying on Hera's original legacy, still claimed to control winds and sold them to seamen as late as the sixteenth and seventeenth centuries.[116] There are similar stories from many other lands. Frazer, for instance, notes:

> Finnish wizards used to sell wind to storm-stayed mariners. The wind was enclosed in three knots; if they undid the first knot, a moderate wind sprang up; if the second, it blew a gale, if the third, a hurricane.[117]

One may well speculate whether the word "knot" used in modern nautical nomenclature is somehow related to the "knots" in all these old legends of saints, sailors, winds and storms.

Various other methods have been tried to conquer demon winds, including throwing a tribal vessel, collectively urinated in, onto the demon. Shooting arrows, using spears, swords, lances and sabers to hack at the invisible foe, all have been tried. People even have resorted to shooting guns and cannons to scare it away.[118]

---

[113] Jennings, *Killer Storms*, p. 179.

[114] Douglas, *Hurricane*, p. 72.

[115] Frazer, *The Golden Bough*, p. 30.

[116] Graves, *Greek Myths*, vol. 1, p. 162.

[117] *The Golden Bough*, p. 27.

[118] Ibid., p. 28.

In more modern times, people have wanted to control the hurricane with science, to try nuclear bombs to blow it away (a bigger gun), which would not work anyway. Cloud seeding has been attempted several times to break up the eye walls and winds, with questionable results at best. The most up-to-date information on the subject is from the science magazine *Omni*. It summarizes:

> Thus far there is still no human technology known that can counterpunch with hurricanes—the volume and energies of the storms are just too much for us. As things stand now, what nature sends spinning from the warm sea, we must meekly accept—as always.[119]

No one seems even to begin to question the wisdom of trying to master or control the great storm. What unforeseen human and environmental retribution might be unleashed upon the planet for so arrogantly tampering with Hurakan's domain?

Forecasting the hurricane is another way of trying to control it— or at least to avoid its destructive consequences. There is an intriguing story combining elements of ancient folklore and modern forecasting. Nash Roberts, the most famous hurricane meteorologist in New Orleans, was a "veil baby"—he was born with the amniotic sac surrounding his body. The folk belief is that veil babies can foresee future events. Sailors in earlier times bought these dried-up sacs and hung them around their necks in hopes of being able to foresee the coming storms. Nash Roberts gained his forecasting reputation by predicting more accurately than the National Weather Service exactly where and when several hurricanes, including Betsy, would make landfall.[120]

We moderns probably pray less regarding the hurricane than did our more primitive counterparts, and our rituals have moved from superstitious to scientific, from beating drums and blowing shells to watching televised satellite shots. Though we still have as little ability to control the hurricane as our ancestors did, because of advancements in technology we are able to observe, track and fore-

---

[119] March, 1994, p. 47.

[120] Nash Roberts, Jr., interview, Jan. 24, 1994.

cast the course of the great storms. An early warning system has in recent times saved many human lives, though property destruction continues to climb. In a scientific sense, we are more conscious of the hurricane; that is, we have more knowledge and technical information—though we seem to have lost touch with its soul, its meaning, its myth.

The assimilation of the hurricane, its trivialization in modern culture—another attempt at mastery—is apparent in novels, movies and documentaries. It is reflected in the names given to motor vehicles and national collegiate football teams, famous drink concoctions on Bourbon Street in New Orleans (made from island rum) and a hard-driving song titled "That's What You Get For Loving a Hurricane." Even the word hurricane itself has been watered down and generalized; it has taken on a generic meaning for almost any potentially destructive wind storm, as well as the word now being synonymous metaphorically with any powerful, passionate, emotional outburst, particularly rage.

Sometimes it seems we have almost mastered the hurricane by absorbing it socially and culturally, yet this illusion quickly evaporates when humans face the real thing in storms such as Betsy, Camille and Andrew. When we try to make the sacred profane, it never really works.

On the Mississippi Gulf Coast, where Camille hit in 1969, the impact of the storm was so great it literally has changed how people measure time. They refer to historical events as "before Camille" or "after Camille." This terminology is used in precisely the same manner as B.C. and A.D. A young couple from Patterson, Louisiana tell how, after Hurricane Andrew destroyed their home, blowing the roof off, it had such a profound effect on them that they now refer to all events in their life as happening before or after "the hurricane."

After Hurricane Andrew came roaring through the Cajun Country of Southwest Louisiana in 1992, the storm "was addressed directly on road signs and shop windows, talked about as *he,* and in many ways was an almost living presence." One woman, reflecting on the experience, said, "If a god is indeed something that is uppermost in one's mind and put first in our lives, Andrew was a god for a time to some people. He may still be."

Finally, a most fascinating piece of anthropology and archaeology. Among the pre-Columbian Ciboney Indians of Central America, crude round stone carvings were found of figures with holes for eyes and an open, screaming mouth. Two arms curve away from the head, one on top, one on the bottom (below, right).[121]

Dr. Fernando Ortiz, an anthropologist from Havana, thinks these stone figures are "symbols of the most frightening force these early people knew."[122] He believes they are totems of the hurricane itself. Other than the mouth and eyes, they are identical to the hurricane insignia adopted by the U.S. Weather Bureau (below, left).

There is no known intentional connection between the Ciboney Indian stone figures and the hurricane insignia used by the Weather Bureau. The insignia was developed independently in modern times to show the circle as the center eye of the hurricane, and the protrusions to designate feeder band clouds extending out from the center in the counterclockwise spiral of the storm.[123]

---

[121] The description of these carvings reminds me of the simply executed yet powerful woodcut, "The Scream," by the German Expressionist Eduard Munch.

[122] Douglas, *Hurricane,* p. 38.

[123] Walter Copes, interview, Oct. 5, 1993.

So, an image representing the hurricane has mysteriously appeared in the collective psyches of both a primitive tribal people and a modern group of meteorologists, across hundreds, maybe thousands, of years without any logical explanation. Could this be another example of the collective unconscious and the archetypes posited by Jung? Surely it would make a most intriguing case for Sherlock Holmes.

It is also interesting to note that, as we moderns have found it more and more difficult to see the face of god, what is missing on the Weather Bureau insignia, in comparison to the Ciboney Indians' stone figures, is the face. The Ciboneys, of course, had no difficulty seeing the face of god in the power and majesty of the great storm.

3
Psychological Perspective

Societal Ambivalence and the Nightmare

In addition to the psychological responses of humans to hurricanes mentioned in previous chapters, there are a number of other, specifically psychological phenomena, both collective and individual, which relate to the hurricane and its occurrence.

Even before a hurricane actually arrives, there is an approach-avoidance reaction to the coming of the storm. People are attracted and repelled at the same time, as for several days they track the storm that threatens their communities and lives. This duality of response creates a tension of opposites, a powerful excitement: fascination, anticipation, fear. On the one hand, everyone wants to be touched in some way by the specialness of the storm, to feel the power of the awesome beast, and yet, at the same time, they hope and pray in trembling awe to be spared, *not* to be touched by its furious destructiveness. There are always signs of both relief and disappointment when the great storm turns away and visits its wrath upon others.

A New Orleans attorney and poet, Brod Bagert, captures the essence of this feeling experience in the following lines:

> She's alone out there in the Gulf.
> Her black clouds boil
> Like spells in a witch's cauldron.
> Wild as a Cossack dancer
> She whirls tornadoes in her wake.
> She crawls,
> Like a cosmic spider
> She creeps,
> She seeks land.
>
> They say it will hit by morning
> So I tape windows

Gather candles
And wait,
But there is no place to hide.
We have no inventions to tame
This atmospheric bulldozer
That pushes oceans in its path.

In the back yard
Something is wrong with the grass,
The green is not the same.
I have never breathed air like this before!
The pear tree,
Possessed,
Bends hard and shudders in a sudden gust of wind,
Wild wind
That rushes over me
So when I spread my arms
I'm flying.

And I hope it doesn't stop,
I hope she doesn't turn away . . .
Deep inside,
I hope she comes.[124]

Much of the human reaction to the hurricane is marked by ambivalence. When a hurricane comes close to hitting a community,
but misses, people often experience a strange annoyance and irritability for several days afterward. It seems there is almost a re-
sentment that the hurricane chose to go elsewhere. The people are
then left with a combination of undischarged energy and pent-up
anticipation. They have no choice but to return to the mundaneness
of their daily routines. It is akin to what Jung called the regressive
restoration of the persona,[125] only on a collective level. The hurricane is always an extraordinary event.

When a hurricane does hit a community, there is created a rela-
tivization of time and space and activity around its coming, arrival
and leaving. All human endeavors not related to the hurricane and

---

[124] "Hurricane," in *A Bullfrog in Café Du Monde.*
[125] See *Two Essays,* CW 7, par. 254.

survival cease to be of importance. All commercial, social, political, educational and religious activities and events are canceled. A client of mine reminded me that the hurricane changes everything, including the food people eat. Electricity, gas and water are often knocked out during the storm, making it impossible to cook or to store food in the usual ways. People eat differently (out of tin cans) and in different quantities (gallons of melting ice cream) than they would at any other time.

Everything stops, stands still; there is a kind of collective holding of the breath until the great storm passes. Civilization is literally suspended, as if to acknowledge and bow to a power greater than itself. The collective, psychological response of humans to the actual hurricane is not much different today than it has been for thousands of years. We are humbled and reminded of our helplessness, of the forces of nature over which we exert no control.

The terrible aftermath of a hurricane can be psychologically devastating, leaving deep scars upon the land as well as on the bodies and minds of human beings. For example, after Hurricane Andrew in 1992, survivors in Homestead, Florida, kept repeating one word over and over, like a mantra: "War!" It looked and felt just like a burned-out combat zone. Entire neighborhoods were blown away, as if they had been bombed. "People roamed the streets, hungry and frightened. Children were in shock." Four months after Andrew hit, mental health experts in the area reported that storm victims continued to suffer from symptoms similar to those experienced by many combat veterans:

> People are numb and easily excitable. Sometimes the clatter of rain or the whistle of the wind triggers flashbacks. The slightest noise startles them. They can't sleep deeply. Nightmares haunt them.

Statistics indicated that after four months, thirty percent of the people in Homestead still hid under their mattresses. Seventy-eight percent of the children at an elementary school reported they still replayed scenes from the hurricane in their minds.[126] Over six

---

[126] *The Times-Picayune*, New Orleans, Jan. 10, 1993.

months later, hundreds of people "were still just sitting there" in shock, many in a state of depression, many in despair, their spirits and motivation gone, completely sucked away by the storm. Children cried when it thundered or rained. The family stresses in the aftermath of the storm were overwhelming. The divorce rate in the county rose thirty percent. Child abuse reports multiplied. Intact families struggled to cope with everyday existence.[127]

Living through a devastating hurricane can result in Post Traumatic Stress Disorder (PTSD). All of the symptoms described in relation to people's reactions to Hurricane Andrew are classic PTSD symptoms: easily startled, restlessness, excitability, flashbacks, anxiety, irritability, depression, difficulty sleeping, nightmares, and so on. Remember that the hurricane had destroyed people's lives, loved ones, homes, jobs and security.

Recurring nightmares about the hurricane are typical: people relive the traumatic event over and over in their minds and in their dreams. It seems to be the psyche's way of gradually burning out the overwhelming psychological effects of the experience. Another way to look at it is that the reccurring PTSD nightmare keeps working at the trauma material, breaking it down until it can be integrated or the psyche is ready to accept it. This usually is signaled over time by a decrease in the frequency and intensity of the dreams, or, as Harry Wilmer has demonstrated with the traumatic dreams of Vietnam veterans, there are shifts and changes in the actual dream content, subtle at first, which signal a potential for healing and recovery.[128]

The PTSD hurricane nightmare is one of three types of hurricane dreams. It follows the typical course of dreams resulting from traumatic events such as war, rape, mugging, shooting, and other life-threatening situations and natural catastrophes. The other two types are anticipatory and symbolic.

---

[127] Ibid., Feb. 7, 1993.
[128] See *Dreams of Vietnam.*

Anticipatory and Symbolic Dreams

The second type of predictable dream is where people have anticipatory dreams of hurricanes as real ones are approaching. These
dreams are usually compensatory in nature, a reaction, as the person is dealing with a combination of anticipation and fear.

The third type, and the most interesting psychologically, involves dreams of hurricanes by people without any direct experience of potential, approaching or existing hurricanes. In these
cases, it seems the psyche appropriates the image of the hurricane
for its own symbolic purposes.

The dreams that follow have been gathered from various
sources, including friends, relatives, analysands and colleagues. I
received hurricane dreams from individuals living in Louisiana,
Mississippi, Florida, Georgia, Texas and Montreal. Most of the
dreams, as one might expect, come from the Louisiana/Mississippi
Gulf Coast region where I live, and where the hurricane is geographically most prominent. Though I cannot prove it, I do believe
that the image of the hurricane can and does appear in the dreams
of people in many other regions, though perhaps not as frequently.
Communications technology has made people everywhere aware of
these storms, not just those who live where they occur.

A young woman in her thirties presently living in Georgia, who
saw me about a dozen times over three years, dreamt of a hurricane
after consulting with me on a visit home. The dream came at a piv-
otal point in her life and at a crucial time in her analysis as she was
working through transference-countertransference issues with her
female analyst. She was trying to decide whether it would be best
to stay with her analyst or switch to a male. She was also battling
an immobilizing depression which she felt had the potential to destroy her completely.

She dreamt she was in the old shed behind the house where she
grew up. There was a tree growing through it. A horrible storm was
raging. She and others in her family were hiding behind the tree,
hunkered down, trying to avoid the rain driving in on them like

bullets. The rain finally stopped as the young woman wondered, "Is this a tornado dream or a hurricane dream? If it's a hurricane dream, I have to tell David." (She knew I was working on this material.) She continued:

> When we came out, the weather was absolutely perfect. Suddenly it occurred to me that this was only a calm lull, the eye (I?) of the storm. This was definitely a hurricane and it was my task to get everybody inside before the next round hit.

When the young woman returned to Georgia and told her analyst about the dream, her analyst asked her to describe me. I am 6' 4" tall and weigh around 260 pounds. She said, "He is like a great big, cuddly bear. He would fill that door if he came in now." The young woman's consultation with me had been a brief respite, a calm lull, from the horrible storms of her process and depression, the implications of which, like the hurricane in her dream, went back to her early childhood and affected many others in her family. The young woman and her analyst realized she felt protected by my strong, nurturing anima, the "great bear" energy she associated with me and which until this time had been the missing element in her analysis. Synchronistically, her analyst had written her thesis on bear energy and understood perfectly what was needed.

Through this chain of events precipitated by the hurricane dream, this woman had a transforming insight which aligned her and her analyst in a powerful experience of the Self, confirming the therapeutic process as being on the right track. She associated the tree growing in the shed with the tree of life, another Self symbol. Other implications are that her individuation journey requires better ego defenses to protect her from the destructive aspects of her psychic storms—the bullets that could kill her and others. She is required to see clearly the nature of the psychic storm, the hurricane, not to mistakenly underestimate it for a lesser storm, a tornado. The eye of the storm is not the I of the ego. She should also be aware of the dangers of a false sense of security, by which she might naively assume the storm is over. As well, her positive transference to me should not be mistaken for the answer to her dilemma, when it is only a transitional part of her work. Her task at this point is to defend, preserve and protect her consciousness and her family's until the storm passes and the sky truly clears.

It is significant to note how the psyche incorporates both me and my hurricane research into the text of her dream, using them to emphasize the Self's greater agenda, pointing the way to what was essential to her analysis but missing until that time. The dream emphasizes the broader archetypal implications of the hurricane, which reflect both the destructive and creative potentials of her situation. In contrast, the more limited though dangerous tornado, a localized disturbance, can quickly rise up, expend its energy and disappear. It is much like a complex which is activated in the psyche, discharges its energy and then becomes dormant again. It, too, seemingly disappears. The young woman's psychic situation required and called forth an image of the Self in the mandala form of the hurricane, which assisted in the necessary reordering and healing process serving the totality of the psyche, not just the ego.

A woman in her fifties dreamt of "looking at a map showing a hurricane moving up the Mississippi River, then becoming stationary . . . straight across from our house." She had another hurricane dream seven months later, where it was heading north up the Gulf Stream to Canada. These dreams came at a momentous crossroads in her life. Within two years she had divorced, moved out of "our" house, moved into her own house in the city (image of the Self), and pretty much completely transformed the geography of her life.

The hurricane in the first dream, sitting outside her door on the river, is calling to her, perhaps threatening her. She is conscious of it on her psychic map. The hurricane is an emissary of the Self; it is urging her to come out and deal with her individuation with all its conflicts and dualities, pains and pleasures, gains and losses, creative and destructive aspects. The second dream reiterates and emphasizes her need to face the tumultuous changes necessary in her life. Otherwise, this individuation opportunity may head north and pass her by forever.

A middle-aged man dreamt:

I was at a beach resort with high sand dunes. There is a hurricane coming as I and others are putting black dirt with roots in it from the shore into bags (like sand bags). This is going to help somehow when the storm comes. I wonder if it will be enough, if it will help, will it make any difference?

At the time of this dream, the man was terrified that the chaotic forces in his life were about to destroy him, his marriage and his family. Did he and others around him have enough rootedness and grounding to survive the winds and waters of the rising unconscious, or would it "make any difference?" Would his world, his persona, his security, be blown away by the Self on account of his individuation? Would he be able to hold the high ground—consciousness and a moral position? The storm did hit, the roots held, his efforts were not in vain; he, his marriage and his family survived and his journey continued. He found a new strength and confidence, a new depth and grounding in the Self.

An adult woman, dominated by a terribly conflicted relationship with her father, dreamt of being with him as a hurricane and its storm surge were moving up the Mississippi River. The hurricane seemed to become a huge water spout. In a second scene, she was with her mother trying to protect herself and her son from a smaller tornado.

Her individuation appears to require that she first deal with her powerful father complex which feels awesome and monolithic to her. Secondly, she must deal with her mother complex—the smaller tornado. The greater Self reflected in the image of the hurricane dominates the psychic scene and holds the energy potential either to redeem or destroy her. The storm surge warns of overwhelming unconscious material which may swamp her consciousness. The dream points to disturbing psychic energy around both of her parents and the need to provide ego protection for herself and her developing positive animus, imaged in the son.

A single woman in her early forties, who had seen me in analysis weekly for almost four years, dreamt of a hurricane at the most crucial point in her life, when every major aspect of her existence was changing in a fundamental and dramatic way. Her history involved many early developmental wounds. As a child, her mother often severely beat and berated her. She was sexually molested by a male neighbor. Her father was critical and distant. As an adult, she had a series of unsuccessful relationships with alcoholic, abusive and unavailable men. Much of her therapeutic work had been concerned with the containment of typical narcissistic, borderline aspects of the wounded Self.

At the time of the dream, she was considering buying a house of her own for the first time, and she had started a relationship with a man who had the potential for intimacy and commitment. She was also reassessing her career and work situation, her parents had broken off communications with her for being honest, her health was very fragile, her biological clock was ticking, and she discovered she was pregnant with twins.

In the midst of all this, she dreamt:

> I'm in Florida on the Gulf. I'm working with children from the hospital. I'm walking on a pier out in the water. It's a stormy afternoon, it's getting darker. I tell others, "It's gonna be worse than expected, need to evacuate, lots of flooding, need to clear the animals out, need to evacuate the kids from the hospital." I'm on duty, some people are leaving in boats, others are complacent. I go to check the animals. The dock is separating from the building. I get to one house with people and a little dog. In the next house there is a cat, I put it on the second floor, then I decide to take it with me. The situation is worsening. Most people are leaving. I thought, "We're having a hurricane!" My boyfriend is on the mainland waiting for me. He is annoyed and worried. I have a sense I'll get out and be okay.

The dream indicates things are going to worsen before they get better, get darker (more unconscious) and stormier (more confusing), but she knows what is most important, what she needs to do— to save the animals (instinctual life) and the sick children (the wounded, yet potential life for the future). Her psychic ground is shifting and separating from old structures to possibilities of a new life. She takes the cat (the instinctual feminine) with her, does not reject it because of her own terrible mothering. She recognizes the reality, the gravity of what is happening (holding on to consciousness in the crisis). It is a hurricane and its transformative potential is immense, representing the possibilities of complete disintegration into chaos (she loses everything) or of a chance for coming together, healing and completion in her life in a way she has never known before. Her boyfriend is on safe, conscious ground (the mainland) waiting for her. The final sense of the dream is hopeful; she is optimistic that she will survive, unite with her lover, save the animals, the children and herself.

In the shaky, succeeding months after the dream, she struggled but she built and moved into her own new house. She and the man married, her parents have resumed respectful communications with her, she chose to give birth to her babies and, yes, she and the twins are doing just fine! She has done remarkably well coping with the swirling winds of her hurricane journey. She is happier, more content and fulfilled at this time than she has ever been as she embraces the abundance of her new life.

Stories of hurricane dreams do not all end so well. A sixty-three-year-old woman dreams of a horse in a field and a hurricane coming, and says, "I really think my whole life would have been different if I could have conquered my fear of horses when I was a child." She is trapped in a miserable marriage with an abusive, alcoholic husband whom she is afraid to leave.

The fact that she dreams of the hurricane and the horse from her childhood seems to indicate that the Self is giving her another chance to address and work through this essential psychological-developmental material. She must muster the courage to face and overcome her fundamental fears, which have prevented her from living her own life. The hurricane is coming to hold her accountable with either success and redemption or failure and despair.

The hurricane dream of the young man mentioned in the preface came after he had been in analysis with me for almost a year and a half. His presenting symptoms involved clinical depression and suicidal thoughts. He was on Prozac, had hand tremors associated with tension and anxiety, was obsessive and perfectionistic. He was

a good student and had talent as an artist. He often dreamt of tornadoes and water spouts, and he was fascinated with weather phenomena. His hurricane dream, wherein the house stays together and
holds against the storm, occurred three months before the death of
his grandmother from cancer and the sudden, unexpected death of
his own mother from a heart attack the very next day.

The hurricane dream warned of a great psychic storm and an
early opportunity for individuation more profound than the regular
anxiety storms of adolescent adjustment, imaged by his many tornado and water spout dreams. He had only one hurricane dream—
the big one. The dream prognosis is good. His psyche in the image
of the house holds together and survives the storm. He is strong
enough and resilient enough to handle the pounding waves of wind
and water from the unconscious.

In reality, he has handled the devastating circumstances excep-
tionally well. He has balanced his grief, living changes, school,
swim team, art and a new girlfriend with a depth and maturity far
beyond his seventeen years. At this time, he is no longer clinically
depressed and most of his previous symptoms are gone. He no
longer needs antidepressants and has a hopeful, positive sense of
investment in his life and future.

So often, hurricane dreams foreshadow great challenges to individuation—resulting in missed opportunities and failure or in the
successful integration of essential psychic material.

A thirty-five-year-old woman dreams of "the soft rain in the
early stages of a hurricane which will result in a massive flood.
Buildings will be covered to their rooftops." She dreams this at a
time when she is feeling inspired and compelled to write, "If I don't
write this novel now, I will never do it—the time is now." She must
juggle her roles as wife and the mother of young children with this
demand from within. The Self, once again in the image of the hurricane, the deceptively gentle "soft rain," is encouraging the creative,
but if it is unheeded, it can result in consequences of the most destructive nature, flooding everything in her psychic neighborhood.

The commonality in all of these hurricane dreams, and others I have found, points to the appearance of the hurricane at a crucial time in the dreamer's life. The specific content of the dreams is, of course, personal, yet the presence of the hurricane image is framed in an impersonal, recurring process, that is, in an archetypal pattern.

The prevailing archetype appears to be the Self imaged in the mandala form of the spiraling hurricane. The implications of this specific mandala image are rooted in the organizational principles of the primitive, awesome energies of nature on a grand scale. There always seems to be great potential—unintegrated, raw psychic energy—available with the appearance of the hurricane image in these dreams, and just like the actual hurricane, it cannot be controlled by the ego or the collective. We humans, internally and externally, become the subject of the great object.

Dreaming of a hurricane can signal the opportunity for the most creative, transforming experience of our lives or it can toll the bell for the most overwhelming destruction we will ever know—all in the name of individuation.

Finally, there is a most remarkable dream of a fifty-two-year-old woman, dated January 1, 1990 (New Year's Day, the birthday of all new beginnings). In her dream, God speaks directly to her from the eye of the storm, a hurricane, just as Yahweh did to Job and Ezekiel in the Old Testament. In her words:

> I warn them (other people) that a terrible storm is approaching although it is so huge we don't stand much of a chance. [The storm hits.] I began to think, "So this may be the end of the world. I hadn't expected it to be this way—so violent. I hadn't expected God to be so vicious." Suddenly a strong, loud, distinctive voice interrupts my thoughts and says, "I can be vicious" or "I am vicious." The voice of God seems displeased with my actions.

She then offers excuses and self-justifications for her life, just as Job did. The voice counters each excuse, each plea and explanation. She continues, "I am disappointed and very upset that God isn't satisfied and wants me to change. Exactly how isn't clear, and I resent it. I am very frustrated." She realizes in the dream that she is dreaming and that it is a message from God.

This woman had only begun recording her dreams three months earlier. She had not read anything at the time by Jung and had never heard the term "authoritative voice." When she was later reading Jung and came across the term, she was startled. She entered Jungian analysis in the spring of 1992. She sums it all up:

> The scene remains the most vivid I have ever dreamed. It remains the most disturbing, fearful, shocking dream I've had. I remain filled with awe when I think of it.

The hurricane, God and the Self are so intermingled in this dream and its effect on the dreamer that they are almost indistinguishable from each other. They truly come together as one symbol with a powerful, numinous aspect, and the archetypal quality of the images is unmistakably "Self"-evident, so to speak.

After writing this section, it seems appropriate, begging Shakespeare's pardon, to loudly proclaim: "Hurricanes are such stuff as dreams are made on!"

Synchronistic and ESP Phenomena

Hurricanes have also been found to be directly associated with ESP and synchronistic phenomena.

In the unnamed hurricane of September, 1947, which slammed into Waveland, Mississippi, a young woman at the time was sound asleep in the early morning hours in a house on the beach, when she had the following experience. "Someone grabbed me by the right shoulder and shook me extremely hard. I sat bolt upright, expecting to see my girlfriend. No one was there."

She got up and found her aunt and girlfriend. Both assured her that they had not awakened her. They quickly realized the hurricane had not gone to New Orleans as expected, but was coming ashore in Waveland. Water was rising rapidly as a neighbor came to the door to tell them to evacuate. They moved to higher ground where, ten minutes later, they watched as the tidal wave completely washed away their house, leaving nothing but the concrete steps and bathroom fixtures. They had escaped just in the nick of time.

If this woman had not been mysteriously awakened, she and the others very likely would not have been ready to escape when the neighbor arrived; they could easily have been swept away and drowned. In many traditions angels are the messengers of the gods as intermediaries in human affairs. As it happens, this woman's name was Angela.

Another woman reported that during Hurricane Camille in 1969, her watch and a friend's both stopped at exactly 12:10 a.m., the precise time that the hurricane struck the Mississippi Gulf Coast, and that her friend's mother died in New Orleans.

The night of the hurricane, this same woman dreamt that her six-year-old son was safe and secure with his grandmother in Ohio, where he was staying at the time. The grandmother later reported that at midnight that night her living room began swarming with bats. They had mysteriously appeared that night and have never appeared again. It should be noted that, at this same time, the woman in Mississippi and the rest of her family were miraculously escaping the worst of the storm as their house was literally being swept away in the darkness.

A more recent ESP experience occurred when Hurricane Andrew hit southwest Louisiana on August 25, 1992. A woman in her sixties, who had lost her husband five and a half years earlier, weathered the storm alone in her house in Thibodeaux. This was the first time she had ever been alone in a hurricane. She was somewhat nervous and fearful by nature. She describes what happened as the winds increased and the storm came upon her:

> There seemed to be a presence in the house with me that was very warm and friendly. I addressed it as if it were my husband. . . . I had a strange feeling of being safe, comforted and not alone.

She made it through the storm without any difficulty. Was the comforting visitor the spirit of her deceased husband, her imagination or some other phenomena? Whatever it was, it was a powerfully significant experience for her.

Here are some of Jung's comments on synchronistic and/or ESP phenomena:

By far the greatest number of spontaneous synchronistic phenomena that I have had occasion to observe and analyse can easily be shown to have a direct connection with an archetype. This, in itself, is an irrepresentable, psychoid factor of the collective unconscious.[129]

When analysing unconscious processes I often had occasion to observe synchronistic or ESP phenomena, and I therefore turned my attention to the psychic conditions underlying them. I believe I have found that they nearly always occur in the region of archetypal constellations, that is, in situations which have either activated an archetype or were evoked by the autonomous activity of an archetype.[130]

As Rhine's ESP (extrasensory perception) experiments show, any intense emotional interest or fascination is accompanied by phenomena which can only be explained by a psychic relativity of time, space, and causality. Since the archetypes usually have a certain numinosity, they can arouse just that fascination which is accompanied by synchronistic phenomena. These consist in the *meaningful* coincidence or two or more causally unrelated facts.[131]

Sometimes the hurricane manifests as an image both in a person's dreams and in an ESP experience.

The writer and astrologer Alice O. Howell, now in her seventies, weathered the famous hurricane of 1938 which hit New England. She was fourteen years old at the time, in a boarding school in Providence, Rhode Island. It was a most terrifying experience for her. A little more than a year before, she and her mother had been in California visiting a psychiatrist friend who was interested in ESP phenomena. One evening they met a woman psychic in San Diego. The woman asked Alice's mother if she had a brother who lived out in the country. Her mother said yes she did. The psychic then asked if he was in the lumber business. Her mother responded no, not at all. "That's odd," said the psychic, "because I see this house . . .," and she proceeded to describe Alice's uncle's house in

---

[129] "Synchronicity: An Acausal Connecting Principle," *The Structure and Dynamics of the Psyche*, CW 8, par. 912. The term "psychoid" refers to the essentially unknown but experienceable connection between psyche and matter.

[130] "An Astrological Experiment," *The Symbolic Life*, CW 18, par. 1190.

[131] *Aion*, CW 9ii, par. 287, note 1.

Dublin, New Hampshire, to perfection, except for the fact that she saw it "surrounded on all sides by stacks and stacks of cut logs." Alice and her mother shook their heads in bewilderment.

The psychic's seemingly inaccurate vision came true a little over a year later when the 1938 hurricane mowed down and flattened the woods all around her uncle's home.

Alice also tells of terrifying recurring nightmares of being at sea in a hurricane in the black of night, or being threatened by a huge tidal wave. The dreams started not long after World War Two began, and continued until 1945 when she met her life-long mentor. Shortly after that meeting she dreamt that a tidal wave over 300 feet high was coming toward her. "It was a towering, gray-green monstrosity." She began to run, knowing full well that she could never escape; then she turned to face death, saying her mentor's name. In that instant the tidal wave turned into a great gray, silent cliff. Up high she could see that green turf was spilling over the edge and birds were flying on and off. From that day forward she has never again dreamt of hurricanes or a tidal wave.

Alice reports that before this dream her life was in a state of constant turmoil and emotional distress. This was imaged by her recurring nightmares of being threatened by a hurricane or tidal waves. These indicated psychic flooding by the overwhelming wind, water and darkness of the unconscious. She says that meeting her mentor was a crucial turning point in her life. It restored a sense of meaning for her and facilitated a fundamental transition to a more conscious position, putting her on her individuation path. This is imaged in her "big dream" by her willingness to face her own death. The ego-persona identifications had to die. The speaking of her mentor's name at the instant the destructive tidal wave transformed into the solid, secure cliff mirrors and affirms the significance of the mentor in her life. The mentor represents aspects of the Self that Alice must eventually make her own.

The combination of her willingness to face death and to follow her mentor were the ingredients of the attitude necessary to transform the overwhelmingly destructive, unconscious material of the mother of all tidal waves into the well-grounded consciousness of the cliff capable of supporting life. The green turf images the potential for hope, peace and abundance rooted in the rock-solid consciousness of reality. The birds flying on and off the cliff indicate the potential for a spiritual dimension in her life balanced by a freedom to explore and yet connected to the solid earth.

In short, the big dream tells Alice that she must face her shadow, her stormy unconsciousness, at the same time as she establishes a conscious connection with the Self, represented by her mentor. To do this requires disidentification from the existing ego-persona complex. She cannot run away. She must face her fears and accept that some of her old familiar psychic structures and attitudes have to die; which is to say, she must be open to transformation.

The dream, her mentor and, indeed, Jungian psychology, did take root in Alice's life, and she has not lost that core sense of meaning in the many years since, "despite every kind of test."[132]

Bob, a man from Louisiana, died on Thursday, July 5, 1979, at the age of fifty-seven. His death resulted from injuries received the week before in an automobile accident. Bob owned a shell dredging company operating in Lake Pontchartrain out of Madisonville, Louisiana. According to Bob's adult son, Sid, Bob knew he had suffered serious injuries, but he did not realize they were life threatening until a few days before his death in the hospital. He was put on morphine for the pain. Bob was also a very dynamic, energetic man who had struggled all his life with alcoholism.

On the day before his death, Bob was informed that his right arm had to be amputated because of the growing infection. He was heavily sedated and in a delirious state. Several times, with a sense of urgency in his voice, Bob told his son that a hurricane was coming and that he needed to get ready to deal with it:

> Sid, batten down the hatches; there is going to be a huge storm; make sure the tugboats and barges are tied off; make sure the dredging equipment is taken care of; get ready for the storm.

---

[132] Thanks to Alice O. Howell for this communication.

Bob died the next day.

Less than a week later, and rather unexpectedly, a hurricane constellated in the Gulf of Mexico south of New Orleans. Though it was not one of the most powerful storms with wind gusts of 60 to 70 miles an hour, it did kill one man, flooded coastal parishes and knocked out electric service to 53,000 homes.

The storm's eye, according to Sid, passed directly over, if not very near the site of his father's dredging company in Madisonville. The storm did not begin developing until several days after Bob's death. He had no direct conscious way of knowing of its existence before he died. The last piece of factual information in this story is that this hurricane was the first storm named after a male by the National Weather Service, and yes, it was named "Hurricane Bob."

The synchronicities in this story abound and combine with a number of archetypal themes already associated with the hurricane. Bob did have foreknowledge, somehow, of the actual coming hurricane. The hurricane did, in external reality, potentially threaten the dredging company as Bob had predicted. His warning to his son to batten down the hatches was good advice on a practical business level. The fact that the hurricane was named Bob is a curious and eerie coincidence.

The archetypal theme of death permeates the story. Bob, at the time, was facing his own personal death. The hurricane did eventually kill one man. Was the hurricane image in Bob's psyche an angel announcing his coming death? Was it a messenger from God coming to escort his soul away from this earth? Was the hurricane image an archetypal echoing of the storm god, Wotan, and Bob's stormy personality, combining and merging in the same image at this crucial time in his life? Remember that Wotan in myth literally represented the hurricane. He ruled by means of magic, and could change shape at will. In modern psychological terms, Wotan's magic and shape changing would be translated as the relativizing of normal time and space dimensions associated with all ESP and synchronistic phenomena.

Bob's story raises additional theoretical questions on the personal psychological level. Was the urgent message from Bob really meant for Bob himself? Was it pointing by metaphor to his need to get his personal business in order, as they say, before his impending death? Was the hurricane image an emissary from the Self designed to break through whatever degree of denial (alcoholic or otherwise) remained in his assessment of his situation? Or was the message meant for his son, Sid, to get ready for "the storm" which would come into his own life after his father's death?

A case could be made for all of these possibilities, and here is one more. Several years later the shell dredging company was attacked by environmentalists for polluting the lake and disturbing the ecological balance. It ultimately went out of business. Was this the meaning of the storm in relation to the business, which Bob could somehow foresee and so was trying to warn his son and others of the threat to their future and livelihood?

The multiplicity of ESP and synchronistic possibilities in this case is fascinating to consider. The combination of the psychic image of the hurricane, Bob's death, and the actual hurricane, presented a powerful constellation of energy on a subjective as well as an objective level. It is impossible to determine what factors influenced, contributed to or caused what other factors to occur. What is clear is that the occurrence of these events goes far beyond random coincidence. It is further evidence of synchronistic and ESP phenomena occurring in direct relation to the existence of both an imagined and an actual hurricane.

In the passage quoted above, Jung states that "ESP involves a psychic relativity of time, space and causality." Elsewhere he points out that the archetype of the Self "acts like a circumambient atmosphere to which no definite limits can be set, either in space or in time."[133] The point here is that hurricanes are an autonomous activity, both physically and psychically. They are also associated with ESP and synchronistic phenomena which are, as stated, themselves closely associated with the archetypes.

---

[133] *Aion,* CW 9ii, par. 257.

Thus a good amount of material on the hurricane, meteorological, mythological, anthropological and psychological, points once again to the central archetype of the Self.

Transformation Experiences

The experience of the hurricane, like other experiences of a numinous, archetypal nature, brings out the best and the worst in people. Some individuals respond with unbelievable generosity, compassion and heroism: sharing food and shelter, intimately comforting and helping total strangers, risking their lives to save others. Other people respond with callousness, greed and exploitation: ignoring suffering, hoarding food and supplies, profiteering, looting and generally taking advantage of the vulnerability of their neighbors.

An artist from Houston, David Martinez, had a hurricane experience when he was seven years old which has permeated his life and his art to this day. In 1970 Hurricane Celia blew through Corpus Christi, Texas. The roof on David's family's home was blown away. David's mother sent his sixteen-year-old brother to cross the street, to see if their neighbor's house was secure. The winds were too strong and they literally blew his brother to the ground as he crawled back to their house. Then David's mother, in an act of great courage and maternal care, proceeded to carry each one of her four children, and his reluctant grandmother, one at a time, youngest to oldest, through the flooding and savage winds, across the street to the shelter and safety of their neighbor's house.

This was a defining moment in David's life. He will never forget the poignancy of that scene. The hurricane has become a recurring theme in his art. He has written and performed a work that includes his experience of the hurricane. He has also created ceramic sculpture around this theme. One moving piece called *To Shelter* (next page) portrays a mother wading through the water, leaning head down against the wind, her arms wrapped tightly around her child. Her hair, the wind, the water and her dress all flow together in a wonderful oneness of form. Clearly David's hurricane experience was of profound significance to his life.

To Shelter, ceramic sculpture by David Martinez

Some people have found their confrontation with the actual hurricane to be the most significant, psychologically transforming experience of their lives. Two Catholic priests, originally from Ireland, survived Hurricane Camille in 1969. They say "it changed our lives . . . possessions and needs are less important," and feel their bond to the community was strengthened immeasurably.[134]

One woman described how she came to grips with what was truly essential in her life only after she was stripped by a hurricane of all her material possessions. She described it as the most freeing experience of her life. Like Inanna-Ishtar's journey into the underworld to her shadow-sister Ereshkigal,[135] which resulted in a spiritual transformation, by being forced to give up everything this woman experienced a total transformation of her life. Much of the monastic rationale for renunciation involves voluntary sacrifice of everything inessential so that one will be free to give oneself completely to the presence of God.

The other side of this coin is that the confrontation with the hurricane has led some individuals to the depths of despair. Those who identify too much with their material possessions are devastated when the hurricane takes everything away. In psychological terms, identification with the persona is an obstacle to individuation because it prevents an authentic connection with the Self.

An example of this appears in Shakespeare's play, *King Lear,* where Lear is caught up in an inflated and illusory identification with his status. He gives away his kingdom to his two evil daughters, spurns his one faithful daughter, and foolishly relinquishes all his legitimate authority and power. The transforming moment for Lear comes in the middle of a storm at night where he apparently loses his sanity. A high school English teacher who wrote to me summarizes the situation concisely. She says, "I personally believe he [Lear] *gains* his sanity here, in the storm. He unclothes and rants

---

[134] *The Times-Picayune*, New Orleans, Aug. 17, 1994.

[135] See Sylvia Brinton Perera, *Descent to the Goddess: A Way of Initiation for Women.*

and raves, and when it's over he sees the truth about himself, his family and what he has done."

It is in and through the storm (which Lear refers to as a "hyrricano") that Lear sheds his clothes (the nonessential persona) and nakedly (authentically, without any pretensions) experiences the truth. The Self (in the nature of the storm) always speaks the truth, whether for good or bad. In Lear's case, it ultimately leads to his death and many others. It is the truth (not necessarily what we want) that sets us free, as Lear learns so devastatingly.

Another literary example of this transformation, though with a happier ending, is in Shakespeare's *The Tempest*. Prospero conjures up an actual hurricane which causes his antagonist brother and several others to wreck on the island where he, his daughter and Caliban have been marooned for many years. The storm shakes everything up, turns everything around, and is the catalyst for straightening out everything in the end. The resolution and happy ending in this play are facilitated as a result of the tempest/hurricane's ability to rip away deceptions and pretensions, so that what is essential, right and true may prevail. This is a playwright's way of describing what is meant psychologically as an authentic connection with the Self. It is no accident that the tempest is a central character in the process of transformation.

The recurring theme of duality often appears around the hurricane. It is as if some people ascend through the vortex of the eye of the storm to a psychological freedom and perspective never known before, while others are sucked down into the vortex and descend into chaotic depths; that is, they are absorbed into the vast ocean of the unconscious.

A fifteen-year-old youth from Louisiana was severely depressed and at the point of despair when he left a note on March 5, 1996, shortly before he made a suicide attempt. In his desperation he instinctively turned to the image of the hurricane to express the depths of the meaninglessness of his life. He wrote:

> Here I am, overwhelming feelings, part of me is numb. Thoughts of what I was, separates me miles from myself. . . . This world is filled

with hate, violence and emptiness. I can no longer bear the pain of the hole of unfulfilled dreams and hopes. I never let on that I was a sinking ship left out in a hurricane. . . .

This young man did not succeed in his self-annihilation attempt. He is now getting help, trying to find hope, trying to find his way metaphorically to the creative, life-giving aspects of the hurricane. One of the potentially redeeming aspects of his situation is that he is a very sensitive poet, and his poetry may yet provide a seaworthy, symbolic vessel for his journey through the storms of life. Poets are always searching for love and meaning and truth, and when they find it, they transform it into a shining moment to share with others. The very act of creating a poem can transport a person out of isolation and connect one with humanity in a deep and meaningful way. There are safe harbors, even for poets.

Jung, as if describing the psychological aftermath of a powerful hurricane, says, "The most intense conflicts, if overcome, leave behind a sense of security and calm which is not easily disturbed, or else a brokenness that can hardly be healed."[136]

---

[136] "On Psychic Energy," *The Structure and Dynamics of the Psyche,* CW 8, par. 50.

Processional cross bent by Hurricane Camille, August 17, 1969

4
The Hurricane As Divine Tempest

Earthquakes, Tornadoes and Volcanoes

To understand better the psychic phenomenon of the hurricane, one should be acquainted with other powerful, natural phenomena and how they might be viewed from a psychological perspective.

The earthquake image, for example, could be seen symbolically as a fundamental shift in the ground of consciousness. An archetypal psychic upheaval that has the potential literally to move the earth on which we stand to a different place changes our conscious standpoint in a radical way. It can easily shake our sense of security, throw us off balance and, if we don't move quickly enough, swallow us up in the grinding maw of Mother Earth.

Psychologically, the quake image may indicate that an over-identification with the persona could be, or needs to be, shattered, values and beliefs realigned and one's view of the world forcibly changed. At the least it would suggest, if not associated with an actual earthquake or traumatic situation, a strong, unconscious challenge to an overly rigid conscious position, or that a necessary deconstruction, the breaking up of consciousness, needs to occur. It might also signal the beginning of a psychotic episode or a mystical process initiated from within or without.

Tornadoes are both similar to hurricanes and very different from them. They are much smaller, can emerge over land or water, always form out of thunderclouds, consist of both earth and water material, and may spin in either direction in both hemispheres. They are usually associated with a larger weather system such as a front or a hurricane. Though they live briefly compared to hurricanes, they are very powerful, intense and destructive, even in their limitedness. They are unpredictable and are therefore more difficult to forecast and track, popping up and disappearing very quickly.

My experience with the tornado image, especially in dreams, is that it occurs more frequently and with more people than does the hurricane. It represents very faithfully a chaotic, powerful, destructive complex that is both conscious (earth) and unconscious (water) and can be triggered by more fundamental, pervasive tensions in the psyche. Though having an archetypal core like any complex, the tornado image appears to emanate primarily from stormy, swirling affect that is unintegrated on the level of the personal unconscious as opposed to the archetypal, collective unconscious.

Marian Woodman sees tornadoes, flash storms and searing fires in dreams as attempts to "alert one to a dangerous situation [that] · can rip the center out of the psychic house."[137] These images can warn the dreamer that a dangerous complex is present and threatening to take control of consciousness, temporarily paralyzing normal ego functioning. Woodman also suggests that "tornadoes threatening the dream ego as it frantically struggles to keep its luggage together" may point to the need for the dreamer to surrender to the unknown.[138]

Volcanoes come from deep within the earth. Hot ash clouds make it impossible for animals and humans to breathe. The superheated lava burns and kills until it cools to become the nourishing ground for new plants and animal life. The volcano image suggests primitive, unconscious, psychic material periodically exploding into consciousness due to pressures deep within the psyche.

Red hot lava is much like raw, archetypal material which is too hot to handle, to humanize. Initially it cannot be integrated psychologically (that is, touched or breathed) until it cools down enough to create solid ground (consciousness) on which to support new life. This new fundament can ultimately be beneficial to plants (the abundance of Mother Nature), animals (the instinctual) and humans (individual consciousness).

In the psyche timing is everything. Volcanoes create and nour-

---

[137] *The Pregnant Virgin: A Process of Psychological Transformation*, p. 50.
[138] Ibid., p. 131.

ish, burn and destroy. Like the archetypes, or the gods, if we get too close to these natural forces in an unprotected way (that is, without adequate consciousness) we can be badly burned (mental illness or psychosis), even destroyed, but if we keep both a respectful distance and a wakeful connection to them, they can, with time, create wonderful new psychic ground and immeasurably nourish our conscious landscape.

These are just brief sketches of what these phenomena might symbolize so that the contrast with the more detailed, amplified aspects of the hurricane may be kept in mind.

As far as we know, Jung never experienced a hurricane. Nor are there any references to hurricanes as such in the Collected Works, although, as noted earlier, he did use the image of the hurricane and other storm winds metaphorically in reference to Wotan, and several times in translations of passages from the Babylonian Creation Epic.[139] There are a number of references in the Collected Works to earthquakes and one dream Jung refers to about volcanoes, but no mention of tornadoes.

Jung did speak about the first time he experienced an earthquake. Addressing a group of doctors in London, England, he told this story to illustrate that fantasies evoked by natural disasters were not necessarily psychotic:

> I once went through a very strong earthquake. . . . I was simply overcome by the idea that the earth was not solid and that it was the skin of a huge animal that had shaken itself as a horse does. I was simply caught by that idea for a while. Then I came out of the fantasy remembering that that is exactly what the Japanese say about earthquakes: that the big salamander [*namazu* in Japanese legend, a monstrous catfish that carries most of Japan on its back] has turned over or changed its position, the salamander that is carrying the earth. Then I was satisfied that it was an archaic idea [that is, an archetype] which had jumped into my consciousness. I thought it was remarkable; I did not quite think it was pathological.[140]

---

[139] See above, pp. 41ff.

[140] "The Tavistock Lectures," *The Symbolic Life,* CW 18, par. 67.

Amplification of the Image

Masculine, feminine or androgynous?

In the chapter on mythology, it became evident that there are almost as many mythological images of the hurricane as feminine (Guabancex, Hera, Tiamat, Harpies, Chimaera, witches, etc.) as masculine (Hurakan, Poseidon, Set/Typhon, Indra, Wotan, Aeolus, wizards, etc.).

The history of the names projected onto hurricanes, as mentioned earlier, ranges from alphabet neutral to women and men and saints and politicians. For my generation, there is a strong association of the hurricane with the feminine because the U.S. Weather Service named hurricanes after women exclusively for twenty-five years, from 1954 to 1979. But of course this is a very short period of time compared to the hundreds, maybe thousands, of years involved in the history of human projections onto the great storm.

The colors of the two hurricane warning flags are black and red. Black is associated predominantly with the feminine: night, primordial darkness, the nonmanifest, the void, the dark aspect of the Great Mother, water, time, dissolution, death, *mortificatio,* destruction, the shadow, the absence of all color, and the *nigredo* (the first or alpha stage of the alchemical opus). It is the color of Pan and the devil.[141]

Red is mostly associated with the active masculine principle: day, the zenith point of color, the sun, fire, emotions and passions, faith, love, joy, fertility and calamity, the blood of life and death, and the *rubedo* (the final or omega stage of the alchemical opus). It is the color of Apollo and Mars, Christ's Passion, Pentecost, the Cardinals of the Church, as well as Set/Typhon.[142]

Now, as we shall see, when the constituent elements of a hurricane are considered, there is in fact a fascinating mixture of masculine and feminine associations.

---

[141] J.C. Cooper, *An Illustrated Encyclopaedia of Traditional Symbols*, p. 39.
[142] Ibid., p. 40.

Water, wind, salt and lightning

Water, according to Erich Neumann, is "the primordial womb of life. . . . It . . . nourishes and transforms." He notes that it is necessary for the survival of all living things, and calls it "the milk of the earth."[143] Jung says water is the prima materia, a totality image, an image of wholeness—the source and grave of everything in the universe.[144] He describes it particularly as a mother image:

> The maternal significance of water is one of the clearest interpretations of symbols in the whole field of mythology, so that even the ancient Greeks could say that "the sea is the symbol of generation." From water comes life. . . .
> . . . In dreams and fantasies the sea or a large expanse of water signifies the unconscious. The maternal aspect of water coincides with the nature of the unconscious, because the latter (particularly in men) can be regarded as the mother or matrix of consciousness. Hence the unconscious . . . has the same maternal significance as water.[145]

Edward Edinger points out that in many creation myths water is the original material out of which the world is made, and that in the alchemical opus it pertains to the stage of *solutio,* the dissolving principle of rebirth and baptism: "Water was thought of as the womb and *solutio* as a return to the womb for rebirth."[146]

Equal in importance to water in the composition of the hurricane is wind. Wind is associated with the spirit, the vital breath of the universe.[147] Jung identifies wind as a symbol for libido, psychic energy, noting that libido "is fructifying [animating, creative] as well as destructive."[148] If wind equals psychic energy, then the winds of the hurricane represent one of the greatest quanta of it known to humans—both creative and destructive. Wind is also as-

---

[143] *The Great Mother,* p. 47.

[144] See, for instance, *Psychology and Alchemy,* CW 12, par. 367.

[145] *Symbols of Transformation,* CW 5, pars. 319f.

[146] *Anatomy of the Psyche,* p. 47.

[147] Cooper, *Encyclopaedia of Traditional Symbols,* p. 192.

[148] *Symbols of Transformation,* CW 5, pars. 422, 428.

sociated with Father, the pneuma, the masculine.[149] It is interesting to note that Jung associates both wind and water with the Holy Ghost.[150] It seems then that water, the Mother uterus, is impregnated by the movement of the wind, the spirit of the Father, which creates the hurricane and/or the Holy Ghost—which pretty much makes them synonymous.

Add salt to the water and it gets even more curious. Paracelsus, combining the medieval idea that man is composed of body, soul and spirit, and the alchemical theory that all metals were composed of Mercury, Sulphur and Salt, declared that "Mercury is the spirit, Sulphur is the soul, and Salt is the body."[151]

Jung associates salt typologically with the function of feeling, and therefore as a symbol uniting two aspects of eros, bitterness and wisdom:

> Tears, sorrow, and disappointment are bitter, but wisdom is the comforter in all psychic suffering. Indeed, bitterness and wisdom form a pair of alternatives: where there is bitterness wisdom is lacking, and where wisdom is there can be no bitterness. Salt [is] the carrier of this fateful alternative.[152]

Salt in its negative aspect is corrosive, spoils things. In its positive aspect it preserves and enhances. Salt is associated directly with Sophia (Wisdom), the ancient co-eternal, eros aspect of Yahweh (the storm god) capable of relating to and loving humankind. Salt is also associated with luna (moon) and the unconscious, and correlates with the feminine principle in multiple aspects.

The pot thickens, as it usually does when cooking with the alchemists. Salt is at times associated with Typhon and the sea monster Leviathan. The alchemist Mylius, writes Jung, "expressly identifies salt with the uroboros-dragon."[153] The identity of sea and salt

---

[149] Ibid., pars. 149f.

[150] "Psychology and Religion," *Psychology and Religion,* CW 11, par. 151.

[151] A.E. Waite, trans., *The Hermetic and Alchemical Writings of Paracelsus,* vol. 1, p. 125.

[152] *Mysterium Coniunctionis,* CW 14, par. 330.

[153] Ibid., par. 338.

is ubiquitous in alchemy, hence salt is "the mother of all things."[154]
According to other alchemists, "The salt of the earth is the soul,"
and some saw it as a cosmic principle, "a spark of the *anima
mundi,*" or as designating the *aqua permanens,* which Jung inter-
prets as "the arcane substance which is at once the transformer and
the transformed, the nature which conquers nature."[155] Indeed, Jung
devotes a very long section of *Mysterium Coniunctionis* to the amplification of salt, both alchemically and psychologically.

To sum up the alchemical point of view, the moistening, flooding, washing, watery aspect of the hurricane *(solutio)* and salt (the
arcane substance) are feminine, but the heating fire aspect *(calcinatio)* and the wind and air aspect *(sublimatio)* are masculine.

Lightning frequently accompanies hurricanes. According to
Jung, in mythology it is equivalent to the phallus.[156] Both thunder
and lightning are most often associated with male gods such as
Zeus and Thor. In an illustrated essay on the individuation process
of "Miss X," Jung includes her painting of an egg/stone being
struck by lightning. He comments:

> The liberating flash of lightning is a symbol . . . used by Paracelsus
> and the alchemists for [the soul]. . . . Lightning signifies a sudden,
> unexpected, and overpowering change of psychic condition.[157]

The spiral and the whirlwind

The spiral movement characteristic of the hurricane is a highly
complex, ancient symbol that appears almost universally in cultures
throughout the world, except, curiously, in Hawaii. According to
Cooper's account, it can represent both solar (masculine) and lunar
(feminine) powers; the air; the waters; rolling thunder and lightning; the great creative force; emanation. As vortex, expanding and

---

[154] Ibid., par. 340.
[155] Ibid., par. 321.
[156] "The Practical Use of Dream-Analysis," *The Practice of Psychotherapy,* CW 16, par. 340.
[157] "A Study in the Process of Individuation," *The Archetypes and the Collective Unconscious,* CW 9i, par. 533.

contracting, it can depict the increase and decrease of the sun, the waxing and waning of the moon and, by analogy, expansion and contraction, winding and unwinding, birth and death.[158]

The spiral denotes fertility and the dynamic aspect of things, the great generative forces. As the whirlwind, it is associated by the Chinese with the manifestation of energy in nature. Spirals and whorls are associated with the spinning and weaving of the web of life and the veil of the Great Mother. The double spiral can represent the coming together of yin and yang—the androgyne. Recent research on hurricanes has found evidence that they sprout concentric eye walls, thus doubling the spiral effect in the storm. The spiral is also connected with the navel as center of power and life.

Marion Woodman says, "The Goddess, in my thinking, is the movement of the spiral."[159] By analogy, she contrasts the circumambulating movement of the feminine with the linear movement of the masculine:

> [The spiral] can move two ways: out toward release or in toward destruction, with the crucial proviso that destruction and release, like crucifixion and resurrection, are one. . . . To find the stillness at the center of the whirlpool, the eye of the hurricane, and not hold onto it with the rigidity born of fear, is what in analysis we struggle to reach. That center I call Sophia, the feminine Wisdom of God.[160]

Woodman feels strongly that the spiral and the eye of the hurricane are predominantly feminine images. She diagrams the destructive, counterclockwise movement of the spiral from the eye of Medusa in contrast to the creative, clockwise movement of the spiral from the eye of the Great Mother (opposite).[161] In doing so, she illustrates almost exactly the contrasting spiral movement, with the eye included, of hurricanes in the northern and southern hemispheres, as well as echoing their tremendous creative and destructive potential.

---

[158] *Encyclopedia of Traditional Symbols*, p. 156.
[159] *Addiction to Perfection*, p. 126.
[160] Ibid., p. 72.
[161] Ibid., p. 32.

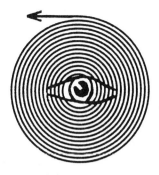

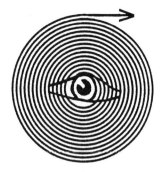

Medusa's eye
Counterclockwise movement
of energy into the unconscious.
Depression
Medusa petrifies

Great Mother's eye
Clockwise movement of energy
toward consciousness.
New energy released
Being feeds Doing

Jung points out that in Eastern, Lamaic rituals, the holy stupas must always be circumambulated to the right, because a leftward movement is evil:

> The left, the "sinister" side, is the unconscious side. Therefore a leftward movement is equivalent to a movement in the direction of the unconscious, whereas a movement to the right is "correct" and aims at consciousness.[162]

Similarly, Woodman notes that in a Black Mass participants circle counterclockwise to invoke the devil, just the reverse of the clockwise movement in traditional sacred rituals.[163]

Thus hurricanes paradoxically contain movement toward both consciousness and unconsciousness, toward good and evil in human terms, toward both individuation and annihilation.

Jung sees circumambulation as a process intended to direct attention toward an inner core, "the patient's first attempt to find a centre and a container for his whole psyche."[164] This is precisely what is suggested by the hurricane image in non-PTSD dreams—the psyche's attempt to call the dreamer to find the true center, the Self,

---

[162] *Psychology and Alchemy,* CW 12, par. 166.
[163] *Addiction to Perfection,* p. 32.
[164] *Analytical Psychology: Its Theory and Practice,* p. 201.

and to let go of the ego-persona identification, the so-called false self. Edinger underlines this:

> A spiral is basically a circular movement toward or away from a central point or axis. Hence it is an apt symbol for the process of individuation, which is a kind of circumambulation of the Self in ever small circles. Where this unconscious dynamism that seeks the center is activated without the ego's being consciously related to it, dangerous or destructive aspects of spiral form appear. . . . If the [ego] is too weak and immature to relate to this central dynamism, it will be sucked down and destroyed.[165]

In another amplification of the spiral image, Marie-Louise von Franz refers to a simple Protestant woman who painted a mandala in the form of a spiral (below). Later, the woman realized that one of the figures in the painting was God himself, and the spiral was an image of the Holy Ghost. Von Franz comments:

---

[165] *Melville's Moby-Dick: An American Nekyia,* p. 135.

That the Holy Ghost is the power that works for the further development of our religious understanding is not a new idea, of course, but its symbolic representation in the form of a spiral is new.[166]

This movement as a connection to divinity is concretely demonstrated by the whirling dervishes of the Sufi religion, who dance in a repetitive spiral as a form of ecstatic prayer—they go into a trance to experience oneness with God. According to a Sufi practitioner I know, they always spin in a counterclockwise direction, which is meant to help destroy egoism and illusion, thus allowing for a more direct connection with, and experience of, the divine. Jung says that the dervishes and other primitive dancers are transported into an unconscious state; in effect, they merge in *participation mystique* with the divinity.[167]

The whirlwind, an integral aspect of the hurricane, is an even more specific image of the spiral. Again, in Cooper's words:

[The whirlwind is] circular, solar and creative movement; ascent and descent . . . regarded as a manifestation of energy in nature, rising from a centre of power associated with gods, supernatural forces and entities who travel on whirlwinds or speak from them. The whirlwind thus becomes a vehicle for the divinity.[168]

Hurakan, Typhon and Set are the whirlwind. Yahweh speaks to Job and Ezekiel out of the whirlwind. In traditional lore, the Holy Spirit comes to the Apostles on Pentecost in the form of a whirlwind. In Amerindian symbolism, the Great Spirit is the whirlwind. Souls can be carried to the next world by whirlwinds, as can people.[169] (Think of Dorothy in *The Wizard of Oz.*)

Recall the woman's dream mentioned earlier, where God spoke to her out of the whirlwind hurricane on New Year's Day. In Jung's anamnesis of the "Miller Fantasies," Miss Miller says that Anaxagoras "makes the cosmos arise out of chaos by means of a whirl-

---

[166] "The Process of Individuation," in C.G. Jung, ed., *Man and His Symbols,* p. 226.

[167] *Symbols of Transformation,* CW 5, par. 481.

[168] *Encyclopaedia of Traditional Symbols,* p. 192.

[169] Ibid.

wind."[170] Jung later comments that "the whirlwind of Anaxagoras was the same divine *nous* [idea] which produced the world out of itself"[171]—an aspect shared with the uroboros. Edinger makes the connection complete in Jungian terms when he states, "The numinous transpersonal Self manifests out of the whirlwind."[172]

The circulatory movement of the whirlwind is not only horizontal but vertical. Edinger writes, "Upward movement eternalizes; downward movement personalizes."[173] This suggests to me that the hurricane is finite, yet eternal; individual, yet divine and impersonal. The combination of these two movements is akin to the alchemical process of *circulatio*. Edinger quotes a passage in the *Emerald Tablet of Hermes* referring to *circulatio*—"It ascends from the earth to the heaven and descends again to the earth, and receives the power of the above and below"[174]—and further notes that chemically,

> *circulatio* refers to the process in which a substance is heated in a reflux flask. The vapors ascend and condense; then the condensed fluid is fed back into the belly of the flask, where the cycle is repeated.[175]

This is precisely what nature creates in the hurricane: warm air ascends as it is heated, the clouds and moisture descend, are sucked back up and heated again and again in an ever expanding and strengthening process. Psychologically, says Edinger, "*circulatio* is the repeated circuit of all aspects of one's being, which gradually generates awareness of a transpersonal center uniting the conflicting factors."[176]

An aspect of *circulatio* relevant here is *coagulatio*, the firming up of a substance. This is promoted by action (diving, churning,

---

[170] *Symbols of Transformation,* CW 5, par. 67.
[171] Ibid., par. 76.
[172] *Ego and Archetype,* p. 89.
[173] *Anatomy of the Psyche,* p. 142.
[174] Ibid.
[175] Ibid.
[176] Ibid., p. 143.

whirling motions—like making butter). Edinger again:

> [The alchemist] Anaximander [says]: "There was an eternal motion, in which was brought about the origin of the worlds." This eternal motion was thought of as a vortex taking place in the "boundless" *(apeiron)*, the *prima materia,* and is very similar to the Hindu myth [according to which the world was coagulated into being by an agitating or churning motion]. Exposing oneself to the storm and stress of action, the churn of reality, solidifies the personality.[177]

It does seem that the hurricane image as a symbol has the great psychological potential to solidify and expand the personality of the individual as part of the individuation process.

Marion Woodman images the *circulatio* as a constantly circulating, creative flow of masculine and feminine energies in the psyche—yang and yin.[178]

Teilhard de Chardin, scientist, philosopher and theologian, in trying to describe the nature of energy, says:

> Hence, we find our minds instinctively tending to represent energy as a kind of homogeneous, primordial flux in which all that has shape in the world is but a series of fleeting "vortices."[179]

Here de Chardin paints a picture of the world being continually created by whirlwinds which gather up, shape and focus energy into ever changing, temporal forms. It is the image of the hurricane as the primal energy, eternal creator of all things.

The eye of the hurricane

One of the unique characteristics of the hurricane is its eye, the center of the storm, where it is possible for humans to reside for a time in a world all its own. It is a temenos, a sacred, mysterious place, both wonderful and terrible.

There are numerous associations and meanings for the image of the eye itself, many of which are relevant to the hurricane. Cooper notes:

---

[177] Ibid., p. 85.

[178] *Addiction to Perfection,* pp. 14f.

[179] *The Phenomenon of Man,* p. 42.

The "eye" as applied to sacred architecture is the opening heaven-wards in the centre of the dome of a temple, cathedral, lodge, or any other traditionally constructed "world centre"; it represents the solar door giving access to the celestial regions.[180]

Here the eye of the hurricane is associated with that part of the sacred temple where the eternal numinous divine makes contact with the temporal finite human. The "solar door" is the opening through which the gods can be present and touch human beings, where epiphanies and theophanies might occur

The eye in alchemy is called the *spiraculum aeternitatis,* an air hole through which eternity breathes into the temporal world. Marion Woodman sees their meeting place as "a vacuum where the personal realm of the psyche touches the eternal, the collective unconscious. It is the place of annunciation, spirit breathing into soul."[181]

Mircea Eliade describes this place in various ways, as the *axis mundi,* the center, the meeting point of heaven, earth and hell, also known as the "navel of the earth" where creation began.[182] Joseph Campbell says much the same: "The navel of the world [is] the umbilical point through which the energies of eternity break into time. [It] is the symbol of the continuous creation."[183]

All these descriptions circumambulate the meaning of the eye as center. Jung says, "The centre is frequently symbolized by an eye: the ever-open eye of the fish in alchemy, or the unsleeping 'God's eye' of conscience, or the all-seeing sun."[184] Referring to a woman's dream of a lens-shaped UFO, he comments:

This image corresponds to the traditional eye of God, which, all-seeing, searches the hearts of men, laying bare the truth and pitilessly exposing every cranny of the soul. It is a reflection of one's insight into the total reality of one's own being.[185]

---

[180] *Encyclopaedia of Traditional Symbols*, p. 62.

[181] *The Pregnant Virgin*, p. 188.

[182] *Cosmos and History: The Myth of the Eternal Return*, pp. 13ff.

[183] *The Hero With a Thousand Faces*, p. 41.

[184] "Flying Saucers," *Civilization in Transition*, CW 10, par. 807.

[185] Ibid., par. 639.

The powerful transformation experiences described by some individuals in relation to their encounters with the hurricane echo the
same kind of coming to grips with the fundamental nature of their
being which Jung attributes to an experience of the eye of God. Joseph Campbell says,

> The center occupies the "highest" or innermost place within the en-
> tire concentric arrangement. The center is the "nameless," the most
> supreme, the oldest, yet is ever-present and continually pours forth
> its energy—it is self-renewing.[186]

Characteristics, once again, which all apply to the hurricane as
image and symbol. As an anatomical image, the eye can also depict
the androgyne as being formed of the oval female symbol and the
circle of the male. The single eye (e.g., the eye of Horus, the third
eye of the Buddha, the Cyclopes and the evil eye) is either symbolic of evil and destructive power or of enlightenment.[187] Plato
says, "There is an eye of the soul . . . by it alone is truth seen."[188]

Jung refers to the moon-eye of Isis and the eye of Horus, the
"Philosophical Eye" and the eye of the Holy Ghost in alchemy, the
eye as seat of human consciousness, as mandala, and the evil eye
which has always been associated with storms.[189]

It is most significant meteorologically and psychologically that
the hurricane *has* an eye—a unique and clearly defined center,
whose implications and amplifications seem to multiply and expand
into the most profound considerations of the interface between the
human and the divine.

The hurricane and Mercurius

There is one theme in alchemy which reflects and synthesizes
more aspects of the hurricane than any other. It is the androgynous,
paradoxical, elusive spirit of quicksilver, Mercurius, who carries
more dualities and oppositions than perhaps any other symbol.

---

[186] Jose and Miriam Arguelles, *Mandala*, p. 60.
[187] Cooper, *Encyclopaedia of Traditional Symbols*, p. 62.
[188] Ibid.
[189] *Symbols of Transformation*, CW 5, par. 408.

The hurricane and Mercurius are not identical, but they do have a great many aspects in common. Some of their shared pairs of opposites are creativity and destruction, good and evil, light and dark, permanence and transience, male and female, father and mother, temporality and eternity, young and old, natural and supernatural, human and divine, sun and moon, wind and water, ascent and descent, visibility and invisibility, moisture and dryness, spirit and soul, death and resurrection, Alpha and Omega. Jung refers to Mercurius as a storm daemon, synonymous with Hermes and Wotan,[190] and associates the spirit of Mercurius with Typhon, Yahweh, Lucifer, Christ and the Devil, as well as with salt.[191]

Like the hurricane, Mercurius is highly changeable and unpredictable, a many-sided trickster phenomenon, and is seen as the one animating principle of all things, representing both the prima materia and the Self, beginning and ending, the final goal of consciousness as well as the middle, the process of individuation. It is co-eternal with the Creator. Mercurius too is androgynous in nature, partaking of masculine red sulphur and feminine Sophia salt—Sol and Luna together.[192]

Jung says Mercurius represents the Self and totality: "The paradoxical nature of Mercurius reflects an important aspect of the self—the fact, namely, that it is essentially a *complexio oppositorum*"[193]—a complexity of opposites, just like the hurricane.

Another aspect of the hurricane shared by Mercurius is that both operate in the *circulatio* in an initially ascending movement, building from the bottom up or from the earth/sea to the sky/heavens. This movement is the reverse of the process of redemption initiated by the divine, which descends from the heavens down to the earth.

Edinger sums up the meaning of Mercurius in Jungian terms, and by analogy the hurricane, when he says "essentially it is the au-

---

190 "The Spirit Mercurius," *Alchemical Studies,* CW 13, par. 250.

191 Ibid., pars. 250, 270f., 283.

192 Ibid., pars. 283ff.

193 Ibid., par. 289.

tonomous spirit of the archetypal psyche, the paradoxical manifestation of the transpersonal Self."[194]

This would be very close to the definitive meaning of the hurricane as symbol, but there is one more aspect of Mercurius which takes us even deeper into the essence of the great storm. Mercurius is directly associated with the uroboros. Alchemists stressed Mercurius's capacity for self-renewal, his ability to self-generate, self-transform, self-reproduce and self-destroy. In the "Aurelia Occulta" text, Mercurius says, "I am the old dragon, found everywhere on the globe of the earth."[195] Jung adds, "As the uroboros dragon, he [Mercurius] impregnates, begets, bears, devours, and slays himself."[196] The closest analogy to the hurricane symbolically is without question the uroboros.

The uroboros: mandala of centroversion

The answer to the earlier question of the hurricane as masculine, feminine or androgynous is yes to all three. It is uroboric in the sense that it contains them all, and trying to separate them is about as futile as trying to find the beginning or the end of the tail-eating dragon or of the mandala circle of the hurricane.

The uroboros, like the hurricane, is its own perfection and wholeness. Erich Neumann points out that mythological accounts of creation "must invariably begin with the outside world, for world and psyche are still one."[197] This is a state of preconsciousness. He goes on:

> The act of becoming conscious consists in the concentric grouping of symbols around the object, all circumscribing and describing the unknown from many sides. Each symbol lays bare another essential side of the object to be grasped, points to another facet of meaning.[198]

---

[194] *Anatomy of the Psyche*, p. 85.

[195] "The Spirit Mercurius," *Alchemical Studies,* CW 13, par. 267.

[196] Ibid., par. 272.

[197] *The Origins and History of Consciousness*, p. 6.

[198] Ibid., p. 7.

The hurricane, as circle, is a symbol of the original complete-
ness. It is self-contained, eternal, in a perfect state of being, independent of any "you" or any "other." It cares not for humans or
rules or morality or civilization—these are all meaningless and ir-
relevant to the hurricane and to the uroboros. They do not need us.

It is interesting to note here, in relation to the awesome tail-eating uroboros-dragon, how often humans instinctively refer to the
hurricane in frightening, prehuman, animal analogies. One magazine writer refers to Hurricane David as a "monster," another calls
hurricanes violent "creatures of the atmosphere." A letter to the editor of a local newspaper refers to Hurricane Andrew as "the Beast."

In Robert Browning's poem, "Caliban Upon Setebos, Or Natural
Theology in the Island," Caliban, the half-man and half-monster of
Shakespeare's *Tempest,* struggles to understand this impersonal,
prehuman aspect of the nature-god he calls Setebos. Caliban fears
Setebos and his capricious use of power. He tries to figure out the
best way to avoid Setebos's wrath, which will select at random
which creatures are to live or die. At one point, Caliban says of
Setebos, "He is terrible: Watch His feats in proof! One hurricane
will spoil six good months' hope." It is in relation to this impersonal matrix of the self-contained uroboros that individual human
consciousness evolves.

Before we become conscious, all is projection, *participation
mystique,* an objectification of the original wholeness—the uroboros. In my opinion, there is no better symbol of uroboric life than
the hurricane. As humans, we need the uroboros, the hurricane, the
circular mandala form/images for the development of our consciousness. The image of the hurricane bores so deeply into the human psyche because it is the image of the Self as uroboros. The
hurricane for humans is an eternal symbol of the call to consciousness, an ongoing reminder of the original oneness out of which we
evolved both biologically and psychically.

In an unpublished poem, "After the Hurricane," Francis Brous-
sard, a Louisiana poet, reflects on the idea of the hurricane as an
impetus toward consciousness. One of the verses reads,

> May the god not be provoked
> by the forgetfulness of man.

These lines image the hurricane as a god whose theophany can be constellated by human neglect. It suggests a causal relationship between people not maintaining awareness of divinity and the appearance of the hurricane. Other lines read,

> The compelling voice.
> It drives you to your destiny,
> to your Self flailed by the wind scented with pine.

Here the poem suggests that our relationship to the divine, in the form of the hurricane, is part of what animates personal destiny and individuation. The implication is that the hurricane forcefully moves us to what is most authentic in ourselves. It serves to connect us with the Self.

A Protestant minister writing about Hurricane Andrew in the local newspaper also makes the point that the hurricane is a call to consciousness, not just to any consciousness, but to consciousness of God, a blessing of the hurricane in disguise. He writes, "I am reminded of the forces outside and within myself over which I exert no control." The hurricane confronts him with his awesome fear, his pride and his delusion, as his "desperate need for God breaks forth into awareness." The hurricane thus humbles the human ego and highlights our ultimate dependence upon the divine. He also points out the grace of heartwarming prayers, emotional support and charity which come in the wake of a hurricane.

Symbols of the uroboros, writes Neumann, "are as alive today as they ever were; they have their place not only in art and religion, but in the living processes of the individual psyche, in dreams and in fantasies"[199]—and in the possibilities of every hurricane season.

The uroboros is a symbol found in diverse times and cultures throughout the world. It reflects all the images of the prenatal, unconscious, primal ocean with the potential (like the hurricane) to

---

[199] *The Origins and History of Consciousness*, p. 11.

create everything. It is the undifferentiated union of masculine and feminine. Its symbolic similarity or kinship to the hurricane is evident in Neumann's description:

> The uroboros, the great round, is not only the womb, but the World Parents . . . in uroboric union, and they are not to be divided [father wind and mother water united in the hurricane]. . . . . The uroboros also symbolizes the creative impulse of the new beginning [like the hurricane spark to creation]; it is the "wheel that rolls of itself" [the self-perpetuating hurricane]. the initial rotatory movement in the upward spiral of evolution. . . . What is meant would nowadays be called spontaneous generation or the self-manifestation of a god [the hurricane creates itself]."[200]

To the alchemist, the uroboros represented the mysterious circulation of chemical substances in the hermetic vessel during distillation, echoing the hurricane as unknowable mystery and movement of the divine. There is inward heat and brooding imaged in the uroboros, like the *tapas* of India, "the creative force with whose help everything is made . . . . from whom it blows, begets, gives birth, moves, breathes and speaks."[201] These qualities are identical to what we know of the hurricane and its image.

The uroboros, like the hurricane, is experienced by the ego as the dark chaotic power of the unconscious, but at the same time as the source of creation and wisdom.[202] This echoes the human ambivalence toward the hurricane as both wonderful and terrible.

Uroboric incest, the final dissolution in union with the Great Mother, always involves death.[203] The hurricane has literally taken many human lives—millions swept out to sea—but in a psychic sense also, human intrigue and identification with the storm signal a kind of absorption, or ego death, where humans become one with the great storm in a powerful *participation mystique,* a loss of consciousness which has the potential to obliterate the individual. The

---

[200] Ibid., pp. 18f.

[201] Ibid., p. 21.

[202] Ibid., p. 23.

[203] Ibid., p. 17.

The uroboros, the snake that eats its own tail,
as the mystic wind rising from the heaving waves.

sometimes suicidal behavior in response to the hurricane suggests this kind of uroboric incest. The young poet mentioned earlier who used the image of the hurricane in his suicide note is an example of this. The regressive pull to reunite with preconscious oneness, to sink into the unformed primal ocean, is sometimes irresistible.

As has been said so often, human contact with the hurricane can renew and transform or it can annihilate. Neumann describes this attraction as the first pleromatic stage of uroboric autarchy (Self-creation): "In many cases, therefore, the appearance of uroboric symbolism [like the image of the hurricane] . . . indicates that the ego is moving toward the self rather than in the direction of objective [collective] adaptation."[204] This is certainly reflected in the symbolic, non-PTSD hurricane dreams examined earlier.

An essential aspect of the uroboros is what Neumann calls centroversion. Centroversion is a separate third process, a *tertium non datur,* different from the process of introversion and extraversion, but fed equally from both. It pulls from inside and outside, conscious and unconscious. Centroversion is a type of homeostasis.

> [It] is the innate tendency of a whole to create unity within its parts and to synthesize their differences in unified systems. The unity of the whole is maintained by compensatory processes controlled by centroversion, with whose help the whole becomes a self-creative expanding system."[205]

Centroversion operates as a principle and a process in the uroboros, in the hurricane and in the human psyche. The hurricane is a wonderful meteorological example of centroversion, a living, swirling, compensating, synthesizing, unifying, self-creating, self-maintaining, expanding system. Perhaps this is why its image echoes in the deepest layers of the human psyche.

Neumann says centroversion in the human psyche causes "unconscious contents to present themselves to consciousness in the form of images. It leads firstly to the formation of symbolic images,

---

[204] Ibid., p. 34.
[205] Ibid., p. 286.

secondly to the ego's reaction to them."[206]

Thus centroversion can be seen as the archetypal principle of the transcendent function involved in the creation and maintenance of viable symbols for the human psyche. Remember that the symbol is a psychic transformer of energy. The hurricane thus not only carries great potential psychic energy, but is also the transforming vehicle by which that energy, through centroversion and the creation of symbols, can be processed, integrated and humanized.

What is so fascinating about the hurricane is that it so perfectly reflects centroversion on a macrocosmic level in nature, allowing humans to speculate on its qualities on a microcosmic psychic level. Neumann talks about centroversion as a biological as well as a psychic phenomenon, but the hurricane precedes both of these, being preconscious, prehuman, preorganic. The hurricane is an archetypal image of centroversion in perhaps its earliest form on the planet Earth. It does seem that centroversion operates as a universal principle and process.

Jolande Jacobi refers to the uroboros as that primeval time when "the Spirit of God moved upon the face of the waters."[207] She thus associates the uroboros with Yahweh before the creation.

Both the hurricane and the uroboros can be seen as mandalas. In general, the mandala image appears as part of the psyche's function of self-regulation, that is, when a disorder in the realm of consciousness calls for a compensatory reordering of chaotic factors. The mandala as a symbol is capable of reorganizing psychic energy, recentering the fragmented individual, turning chaos into cosmos, asserting the principle of psychic wholeness. Hence it often appears at a significant transition time in one's life.

The special characteristics of the hurricane as mandala are its size, movement and power. It images huge quantities of swirling, unintegrated psychic energy, usually coming at a time in the individuation process where one is confronted with conscious decisions

---

[206] Ibid., p. 295.

[207] *Complex/Archetype/Symbol*, p. 141.

that will chart the fundamental course of life for good or bad. Sometimes other mandalas appear in the psyche in response to less profound disturbances on the personal complex level, compensating for situational anxieties, adjustments and adaptations of the ego.

The psychic energy imaged in the hurricane can light up the continent or electrocute the individual. The hurricane image emerges from the collective unconscious, the uroboric origin of ever-renewing psychic energy which can transform nature. The hurricane mandala functions as other mandalas but is of a more primitive nature, touching the primal beginnings of individuation in its most numinous form—divine, savage, impersonal and fearsome.

The Fear of God

Socrates, in trying to know himself, first contemplated Typhon, the personification of nature's destructive power. James Hillman comments that Socrates obviously believes that insight into nature's demonic aspect is the beginning of self-knowledge. He goes on to say that "the nightmare is the experiential base of religion. . . . . through the nightmare, the reality of the natural God is revealed."[208] The nightmare is where we meet the nature god, Pan, hence "panic."

Experience of catastrophic natural disasters often puts humans in contact with Pan, literally and figuratively. The hurricane triggers the nightmare both outside and inside. Hillman points out:

> The God is what he does; his appearance is his essence. In one and the same nature is both the power of nature and the fear of that power. . . . Fear is a call to consciousness.[209]

Fear is a normal reaction to the overwhelmingness of the forces of nature and to facing the unconscious. Hillman associates flight with fear and sees flight psychologically as reflection. He says, "Let us keep reflection close to its prototype, fear. . . . When reflection is rooted in fear, we reflect in order to survive."[210]

---

[208] *Pan and the Nightmare,* pp. lxiif.
[209] Ibid., p. liii.
[210] Ibid., p. liv.

The hurricane forces humans to reflect to survive. It calls us to a consciousness, not to just any consciousness but to consciousness of the divine. The fear of God psychologically is really the fear that the ego will be fundamentally destroyed, that we will lose our individual identity and be reabsorbed into God, the uroboros, the abyss or the Great Mother. It is a fear well founded.

> Behavior that is nature bound is, in a sense, divine; it is behavior transcendent to the human yoke of purposes, wholly impersonal, objective, ruthless. The cause of such behavior is obscure; it springs suddenly, spontaneously.[211]

Remember how at the approach of a hurricane all human endeavors other than those related to the storm cease to be of importance. All commercial, social, political, educational and religious activities and events are canceled.

Hillman also, in a way, explains what is behind the naming of hurricanes. He says,

> The experience of the Gods, of heroes, nymphs, demons, angels and powers, of sacred places and things, *as persons* indeed precedes the concept of personification. It is not that we personify, but that the epiphanies come as persons [such as Hurricanes Camille, Andrew, Betsy and Juan].[212]

Humans instinctively experience the gods in human terms and the gods appear in human guise. It is easier for the infinite to become finite than for the reverse to occur. Thus Hillman:

> When Jung said that we need to learn to fear again, he picked up the thread from the Old Testament—the beginning of wisdom is the *fear* of the Lord—and gave it a new twist. Now the wisdom is that of the body that comes into connection with the divine, as panic with Pan.[213]

There seems to be powerful transforming wisdom that comes to humans as they approach the hurricane experience—a fear and stir-

---

[211] Ibid., p. xix.

[212] Ibid., p. xxi.

[213] Ibid., p. xxxi.

ring of the spirit that has been absent from their everyday lives.

Rudolf Otto describes this fear of God in detail in his classic book, *The Idea of the Holy.* He speaks of the *mysterium tremendum,* the tremendous mystery, the might, the power, the "daemonic" fascination, the "absolute overpoweringness" of getting close to God, the numinous experience. It is the feeling of being submerged, of being but dust and ashes, nothingness. "This forms the numinous, raw material for the feeling of religious humility."[214]

All are humbled before the vast power and majesty of the hurricane. It is truly a religious experience, one that manifests in such concrete images as the bent cross pictured at the beginning of this chapter. This processional cross was in Christ Episcopal Church on the beachfront in Bay St. Louis, Mississippi, in 1969. The entire church building was washed away by Hurricane Camille. Somehow, this cross was left standing, bent and twisted by the force of the wind. The friend who sent me this picture remarked: "This is the only icon I know that has been truly touched by God."[215]

Otto also refers to the "urgency" or "energy" of the numinous object—its vitality, passion, emotional temper, will, force, movement, excitement, activity and impetus. The hurricane surely qualifies as a numinous object. Otto also points to the nonrational aspect of divine nature, the "wrath of Yahweh," devoid of moral qualities, "incalculable" and "arbitrary"[216]—qualities previously enumerated in relation to nature, the hurricane and the uroboros.

Edward C. Whitmont notes that awe and fear are basic characteristics of human nature, part of our instinctual realization of the forever incomprehensible absolute in nature. When we substitute a rational, mechanistic universe, or try to replace a genuine, religious attitude, we constellate free-floating anxieties repressing and suppressing numerous aspects of instinctual and psychic life. We may be equally repressing our "primordial fear" of awe before the irra-

---

[214] *The Idea of the Holy,* p. 20.
[215] Thanks to Rita Breath.
[216] Ibid., p. 23.

tional, ultimate power of life, which we call God.[217]

Every year, no matter how arrogant or mechanistic we become, no matter how far from a genuine religious attitude, nature keeps reminding us, calling us to the primordial fear of God in the eye and face of each hurricane that comes spinning our way.

When it comes, the hurricane constellates the potential for humans to have what the philosopher-theologian Martin Buber calls an *I-Thou* experience. Most of our rational relation to hurricanes is an *I-It* experience. We relate to the hurricane as an object, a "thing" to watch and study and control through our science and technology, but when the numinous, awesome power of the great storm comes close enough, it moves from a "thing" category to a "being" category. It becomes more of a person; it has a unique human name, even a personality. Buber says that in such a situation we are "seized by the power of exclusiveness."[218] We and the storm become special, personal, intimate. We are transformed, ripped out of our isolation into a unity with another. Our relationship becomes one of *I-Thou*.

Buber says relation to a *Thou* is always a direct experience. It is innate and archetypal. Through the *Thou* experience, one becomes *I*. There is no substitute for the living relation with the eternal *Thou* (God). It is the center everywhere and eternal.[219] Contact with *Thou* is contact with the divine. Buber's thesis is that we become most uniquely individual, *I*, through experience with *Thou*. Jung would call it individuation, where ego-consciousness is transformed through experience of the Self. There are also similarities between Buber's concept of *It* and *Thou* and Jung's distinction of "sign" and "symbol." The hurricane image can be an it-sign or a thou-symbol, depending upon the attitude one takes toward it. Is the numinous mana present or not?

---

[217] *The Symbolic Quest: Basic Concepts of Analytical Psychology*, p. 93.
[218] *I and Thou*, p. 7.
[219] Ibid., p. 28.

Synthesis

In this final section I shall focus on two specific areas in hopes of synthesizing the meaning of the hurricane as a psychic phenomenon. First, how does the image of the hurricane parallel the psychic process of human beings and how do we respond to it? Second, how is the amplified hurricane material reflected psychologically, especially in symbolic dreams?

The hurricane begins in the geographic doldrums, a time psychologically of passivity, routine and mild discontent, a time when the ego believes not much is happening. There may be adaptation, but the fire is weak. There is little affect, and enthusiasm for life is muted; everything tastes the same, feels the same. The doldrums are a common habitat for many, whether in adolescence, midlife or old age.

Out of the geographic doldrums a low pressure system develops. This is the time psychically when from this seeming nothingness a low level depression takes form. Normal social and collective activity becomes heavy and burdensome. People walk around feeling "down" with "the blues." Attempts to "psych themselves up" that used to work are no longer effective. They function, but not well.

The meteorological low pressure system then turns into a tropical depression. Psychologically there is a pervasive sense of powerlessness, more like a clinical depression, with difficulty eating, sleeping and coping with life in general. Loss of motivation, isolation and social withdrawal are common. It can also be experienced as ego deflation: loss of persona, status or self-esteem. People feel weighted down, yet empty. They sit in the darkness and terror of their smallness and helplessness. This is the time of the night sea journey, which Jung identifies as "the attempt to free the ego-consciousness from the deadly grip of the unconscious."[220]

The tropical depression then begins to form its winds and clouds into a spiral. It is a time psychically when people will try almost

---

[220] *Symbols of Transformation,* CW 5, par. 539.

anything: quick fixes, affairs, new jobs, aerobics, dieting, hobbies, horoscopes, etc. They are no longer in the doldrums. There is energy and movement, but it is hit-and-miss, not centered or really effective, more like running around in circles, spinning your wheels. The chaos is only beginning to take a mandala form, organizing the unconscious psychic material.

Meteorologically, the tropical depression gradually picks up more heat energy and wind speed until it becomes a tropical storm with a clearly defined center and eye. At this time it is given a human name. The whole process is being fueled by the great, warm ocean waters—the great potentials of the affect-laden unconscious. Things are really cooking now. This is the point psychologically when everything is swirling and up in the air; the individual may feel possessed with passion or rage or the need to act out. The shift is from the passiveness of depression to the activeness of the storm. There is action but it is not well grounded or very conscious. Something must change but the unconscious continues to dominate.

This is the point where, for instance, an affair is mistaken for the answer to one's life, or there is an urge to experiment with drugs; separations, divorces, escapes to the tropics and motorcycles are very attractive. There is a frantic, furious, yet focused quality to the activity. The naming of the storm is a first attempt to humanize and relate psychically to it as a separate other, to deal with it from a conscious point of view.

The tropical storm finally becomes a hurricane. Psychologically the energy from the unconscious is so strong it is staggering, potentially devastating to the very existence of the ego. The threat is not only negative, but positive as well—just like the frighteningly redemptive possibilities of the uroboric Self, or the hurricane. Either way it is a fundamental change, a crucial challenge from the psyche's point of view. At this stage psychic energy can overwhelm like a tidal surge and flood the ego; drug overdoses, suicides, destruction of relationships, even psychosis are all possible.

An appropriate ego response to the hurricane involves separation, a disidentification of the individual from the archetypal image.

Just as land and cold break up and diminish the power of the storm, psychically this means establishing a firmer, more conscious position—thoughtful, observing, watchful, reflective; a moving to higher ground, a more consciously secure, distanced perspective; a cooling down of the affects, working through the complexes involved, not turning over ego control and behavior to chaotic emotions. These are all helpful in dealing with the great psychic energy available in the hurricane.

Fools who stay on the beach and have hurricane parties are psychically flirting with death. They are naive, arrogant and inflated, and will probably be destroyed by the storm one way or the other. They do not heed the hurricane as a call to individuation and so are merely reabsorbed into the uroboros, the great unconscious. Those who heed the hurricane as a call to individuation, who respect, honor and fear it, experience the divine impetus for transformation. They head for higher, safer ground. They protect consciousness until the destructive wind (overwhelming spirit) and water (unconscious flooding) pass. They benefit afterward from the fructifying rains that bring new life, and from the clearing out of old psychic structures to make room for a new creation. They experience the storm's aftermath—the clarity of clean blue skies and bright shining sun—as harbingers of hope and enlightenment.

The human psychological response to the hurricane needs to be like the hurricane fence that allows the wind and water to pass through. We need permeable, psychic structures that can withstand the storm fury. Solid, rigid fences get knocked down, blown into the sea. Resisting the hurricane psychologically with rigid, inflexible ego defenses is a useless endeavor and very dangerous.

Human psychological response to the hurricane could also be like the hurricane lamp that protects the flame from all sides; it keeps the light from being extinguished and blown out. We must hold on to and protect our individual light of consciousness. If we don't, we become lost in the darkness, swallowed up by unconscious forces. The transparent glass shield allows the light out without letting the wind in. We need our individual ego consciousness to see and respond to our many options in order to survive winds and water that care not if we live or die.

Humans should also be like the hurricane straps used in house construction, designed to help hold the roof and walls together by clamping the main construction beams, securing them from all directions. Psychologically we must strengthen our consciousness to withstand maximum psychic winds and pressure from within or without, from every direction. If we are like the little piggy in the fairy tale who builds his psychic house of straw, we cannot expect to weather many psychological storms.

Even if we do use hurricane straps, lamps and fences that can withstand a relatively weak storm, we must always be ready to evacuate when necessary. Psychologically, we must be ready, after doing everything we can to secure our psychic house, to abandon it, always remembering that our true home is our relationship to the Self. If the Self requires us to sacrifice our present conscious ego structure for a new creation, we must be psychologically resilient and flexible enough to do so. No doubt this also requires a special transpersonal grace, but we can and must do our part.

The more experience people have with hurricanes, literally and figuratively, the better they learn to respond to the great storm when it comes. Psychologically, people become more conscious of the Self, its raw, impersonal power, its potentially creative and destructive aspects, as well as the kinds of ego adaptations and responses that are helpful in surviving and integrating the benefits of this huge quantum of psychic energy.

The second area to be addressed involves how the amplified hurricane material is reflected psychologically, especially through dreams. I found that, though the content of the dreams I encountered was very individual and personal, there was a common thread of predominant affect among them all. The common thread is fear; fear of being lost on the journey with the wrong analyst; fear of changing one's life and persona; fear of failing one's partner and family; fear of the father; fear of living out the fullness of one's life; fear of horses; fear of growing up; fear of missing a crucial, creative opportunity; fear of giving up one's self-righteous view of oneself and God.

Each of these individuals had a complex activated in relation to their personal life when they dreamt of the presence of the hurricane. The question then arises, why did the psyche of these individuals choose the image of the hurricane, such a powerful, impersonal, archetypal symbol of the Self? Why didn't the psyche offer symbolic images on an individual ego level? What does this hurricane image compensate for in all of these individuals?

I believe that the psyche chose to activate a personal fear-based complex in order to open the door for that individual to the possibility of the experience of archetypal fear: the universal, awesome, terrible, wonderful fear of God, which is the beginning of wisdom. In psychological terms, this means that the humble submission of the ego to the supraordinate authority of the Self is the prerequisite of the individuation process.

The linking of the ego-Self axis in a conscious way allows for the unfolding of the divine plan. Transitory human fear can link us potentially with the eternal fear of ultimate transformation. Nothing moves us, stirs us up, turns us around, grabs our attention, gets us out of ourselves, more than our relationship with the hurricane. Job was changed forever by his emotional contact with the storm god, Yahweh; he experienced the fear of the Lord directly and personally. Thus Jung says that when he wrote "Answer to Job," he knew "what a storm would be raised."[221]

It seems the psyche wants us to become more conscious, to develop a relationship with the Self, and uses the hurricane image in dreams for this purpose. This implication seems to support Jung's contention that, in some way, God wants and needs a relationship with individual human consciousness. The psyche chooses the mandala image of the hurricane because for that person it is the best symbol to express the meaning intended.

Perhaps the next step in creation requires this special kind of

---

[221] "Answer to Job," *Psychology and Religion,* CW 11, p. 358.

psychic chemistry between the human and the divine. In any case, the hurricane is to my mind the eternal call of the divine to humans to participate in individuation; it is a calling on the most essential, primal level of the psyche.

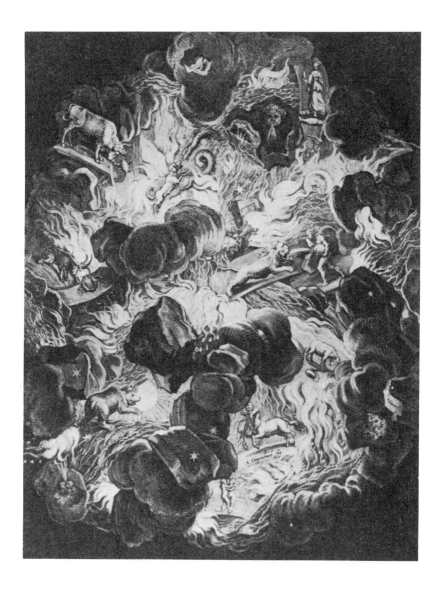

Epilogue
Me and the Hurricane

On October 5, 1993, the night before I was to present my prelimi-
nary research on hurricanes to the Jung Society of New Orleans, I
had a dream. Most of my presentation focused on the meteorological, historical and mythological information I had gathered. I had
not yet explored the psychic meaning of the hurricane. I felt that in
general it operated as a powerful image of the Self, but I did not understand exactly how or why. My conception of the dynamics was
still vague and ill-defined. I sensed I was getting closer to the hurricane's true meaning, but I was not yet there.

Here is my dream:

> I was a passenger flying in an airplane. It was a commercial airliner.
> The pilot was skirting the edge of the outer clouds of a hurricane.
> We were right on the edge high up in the air. The pilot announced to
> the passengers that "right out your window, to your right [we were
> flying clockwise], you can see the edge of a hurricane." It felt like I
> could almost reach out through the window and touch the very ·
> clouds of the storm. It was fascinating and exciting and scary—all at
> the same time.

In retrospect, I believe this dream was a message to me from the
Self about where my hurricane research was at the time. The research was extensive and valid, but mostly an accumulation of external, factual information. This was reflected in my dream by my
being one of many passengers on a collective, mass transit airliner.
My research (observations from the plane) was still from a perspective trafficked by many others. It had not yet become a unique personal perspective (the storm is still "out there," apart from me).
Everyone can see what I see. In the dream I am getting closer (on
the outer edge of the storm). Like in the children's game of finding
the hidden object, I'm getting warmer; I am in the right vicinity and
circumambulating it in the right direction (clockwise). My research

had measured the size and magnitude and breadth of the hurricane, but it had not illuminated its heart, its core meaning. I was still a detached observer (behind thick windows).

Indeed, up to that point in the process, the hurricane *was* still an external object to me, a curiosity. The dream was telling me where I was and where I had to go in relation to my explorations. It was encouraging me to get more involved, to get up close, taste the salty air, truly enter the eye, metaphorically, if I could. In the dream, my desire to reach through the window and "touch the very clouds" tells me that I need to do more than just watch from a distance. My interest was not only in hurricanes as objects; it was also about how what I had come to think of as a "divine tempest" affected me, and how the Self was incarnating on a subjective level through my own psychic involvement. In short, the dream was calling me not to just observe passively, but also to participate in the actual experience of the storm, to feel it inside.

A few months after this dream, I was awakened in the middle of the night for three or four nights in a row. I would be sound asleep, then suddenly I'd be wide awake with a sense of panic and urgency. Each time I awoke, I had a fragment, a new piece of information formulated about the dynamics of the meaning of the hurricane image in the human psyche. Each time I'd get up, turn on the lights and furiously scramble to write down the thoughts and ideas that had come to me, before they slipped away into the darkness of the early morning.

The process was not under my ego control. It was unpredictable, pressured, chaotic and inspired. My wife became a little concerned about my sleeping habits, but after those three or four nights I had miraculously synthesized, piece by piece, the essential components of my dynamic formulation of the hurricane. It felt like it had written itself. Intuitively I knew I had truly penetrated the eye—or it had penetrated me. I had gone to the center, to the heart of the psychic hurricane. It had invaded my sleep and awakened me in the middle of the night, as Yahweh in the Old Testament had called Samuel to do His bidding (I Sam. 3:2-10). It had demanded, like the Holy Spirit with the evangelists, that I write down exactly what it told me, almost literally. In this part of the process I did feel like a passive scribe, the instrument of a greater power.

In some strange way I felt that the Self was dictating to me and through me what to say about the meaning of the Divine Tempest. I hope this analogy does not sound too grandiose. I do not mean to exaggerate my importance or to compare myself with the evangelists. My intent is to illustrate how the dream, the image of the hurricane and my sleepless nights were all used by the Self to process, synthesize and create something greater than my ego-driven activity had been able to achieve.

Time after time, friends, clients and colleagues, without knowing it, would synchronistically send to me the precise piece of information I was looking for. It felt a little spooky, but I was very grateful. I've always been told not to look a gift horse in the mouth. The information I was receiving was a pretty mysterious gift horse, but I still wasn't about to question it.

If the hurricane is truly an image of the Self, a reflection of its nature and significance, then it makes sense that the Self would have a vested interest in wanting to be accurately represented in my material. This is just one more curious piece of the story surrounding the great storm.

Glossary of Jungian Terms

Amplification. A method of interpretation developed by Jung in which a dream image or motif is enlarged, clarified and given a meaningful context by comparing it with similar images from mythology, folklore and religion.

Anima (Latin, "soul"). The unconscious, feminine side of a man's personality. She is personified in dreams by images of females ranging from child to seductress to spiritual guide. A man's anima development is reflected in how he relates to women.

Animus (Latin, "spirit"). The unconscious, masculine side of a woman's personality. A negative animus can cause a women to be rigid, opinionated and argumentative. The animus is personified in women's dreams by images ranging from muscle-men to poets to spiritual leaders. A woman's animus development is reflected in how she relates to men.

Archetypes. Irrepresentable in themselves, archetypes appear in consciousness as archetypal images and ideas. These are universal patterns or motifs present in the collective unconscious, the basic content of religion, mythology, legends and art.

Complex. An emotionally charged group of ideas or images. At the core of a complex is an archetype or archetypal image.

Constellate. Whenever there is a strong emotional reaction to a person or a situation, a complex has been constellated (activated).

Ego. The central complex of consciousness. A strong ego can relate objectively to activated contents of the unconscious (i.e., other complexes) rather than identifying with them.

Feeling. One of the four psychic functions in Jung's model of personality types. (The others are thinking, sensation and intuition.) Feeling is the function that assesses the value of relationships and situations. It is different from emotion (affect), which results from the activation of a complex.

117

Individuation. The conscious realization of one's unique psychological reality, including both strengths and limitations. It leads to the experience of the Self as the regulating center of the psyche.

Participation mystique. A primitive, unconscious connection in which one cannot clearly distinguish oneself from other people or things. This is what lies behind the phenomena of identification and projection.

Persona (Latin, "actor's mask"). One's social role, derived from the expectations of society and early training. A persona is useful both in facilitating contact with others and as a protective covering, but identification with a particular persona (doctor, scholar, artist, etc.) inhibits psychological development.

Projection. A natural process whereby an unconscious characteristic of one's own is perceived in an outer object or person.

Self. The archetype of wholeness and regulating center of the psyche, experienced as a numinous power that transcends the ego (e.g., God).

Shadow. A mainly unconscious part of the personality, characterized by traits and attitudes, both negative and positive, which the conscious ego tends to reject or ignore.

Symbol. The best possible expression for something essentially unknown. Symbolic thinking is right-brain oriented, complementary to logical, linear, left-brain thinking.

Synchronicity. An acausal, meaningful coincidence between an event in the outside world and a psychological state.

Transcendent function. The reconciling new perspective which emerges from the unconscious (in the form of a symbol or a new attitude) after conflicting opposites have been consciously differentiated and the tension between them held.

Transference-countertransference. Particular cases of projection, used to describe the unconscious, emotional bonds that arise between two persons in a therapeutic relationship.

Bibliography

Books

Arguelles, Jose, and Arguelles, Miriam. *Mandala*. Berkeley: Shambhala Publications, Inc., 1972.

Asimov, Isaac. *Words from the Myths*. Boston: Houghton Mifflin Co., 1961.

Bagert, Brod. *A Bullfrog in Café Du Monde*. New Orleans: Juliahouse Publishing, 1986.

Barrett, Norman. *Hurricanes and Tornadoes*. New York: Franklin Watts, 1989.

Bolen, Jean Shinoda. *Goddesses in Everywoman: a New Psychology of Women*. New York: Harper Colophon Books, 1985.

Brown, Billye Walker, and Brown, Walter R. *Historical Catastrophies: Hurricanes and Tornadoes*. Reading, MA: Addison-Wesley Publishing Company, Inc., 1972.

Browning, Robert. "Caliban Upon Setebos." *The Norton Anthology of English Literature*. 5th Edition. Ed. M.H. Abrams. New York: W. W. Norton Co., 1987.

Buber, Martin. *I and Thou*. New York: Collier Books, MacMillan Publishing Company, 1987.

Bulfinch, Thomas. *Bulfinch's Mythology*. New York: Avenel Books, 1979.

Campbell, Joseph. *The Hero With a Thousand Faces* (Bollingen Series XVII). Princeton: Princeton University Press, 1973.

————. *The Masks of God: Creative Mythology:* New York: Penguin Books, 1976.

Campbell, Joseph, and Moyers, Bill. *The Power of Myth*. New York: Doubleday, 1988.

Conrad, Joseph. *Typhoon and Other Tales*. New York: New American Library, 1983.

Cooper, J.C. *An Illustrated Encyclopaedia of Traditional Symbols*. London: Thames and Hudson Ltd., 1978.

————. *Symbolic and Mythological Animals*. London: The Aquarian Press, 1992.

Dalton, Frank. *The Weather*. Hove, Sussex, U.K.: Priory Press Limited, 1978.

de Chardin, Teilhard. *The Phenomenon of Man*. New York: Harper and Row, 1965.

Dineen, Jacqueline. *Natural Disasters: Hurricanes and Typhoons*. New York: Gloucester Press, 1991.

Douglas, Marjory Stoneman. *Hurricane*. New York: Rinehart and Company, 1958.

DSM-IV: Diagnostic and Statistical Manual of Mental Disorders. 4th ed. Washington, DC: American Psychiatric Association, 1994.

Edinger, Edward F. *Anatomy of the Psyche: Alchemical Symbolism in Psychotherapy*. LaSalle, IL: Open Court Publishing Co., 1990.

_____. *Ego and Archetype*. New York: Penguin Books, 1980.

_____. *Encounter with the Self: A Jungian Commentary on William Blake's* Illustrations of the Book of Job. Toronto: Inner City Books, 1986.

_____. *Melville's Moby-Dick: An American Nekyia*. Toronto: Inner City Books, 1995.

_____. *Transformation of the God-Image: An Elucidation of Jung's* Answer to Job. Toronto: Inner City Books, 1992.

Eliade, Mircea. *Cosmos and History: The Myth of the Eternal Return*. New York: Harper and Row, Harper Torchbooks, 1959.

_____. *Images and Symbols: Studies in Religious Symbolism*. Princeton: Princeton University Press, 1991.

Ellis, Edward S., ed. *1000 Mythological Characters*. New York: Hinds, Noble and Eldridge, 1899.

Fradin, Dennis Brindell. *Disaster! Earthquakes*. Chicago: Children's Press, 1982.

_____. *Disaster! Hurricanes*. Chicago: Children's Press, 1982.

Frazer, James G. *The Golden Bough: The Roots of Religion and Folklore*. New York: Avenel Books, 1890 (reprint 1981).

Graves, Robert. *The Greek Myths*: 1. Baltimore: Penguin Books, Inc., 1971.

_____. *The Greek Myths*: 2. New York: Penguin Books, Inc., 1960.

Harding, M. Esther. *Woman's Mysteries: Ancient and Modern*. New York: Harper Colophon Books, 1976.

Hillman, James, and Roscher, Wilhelm Heinrich. *Pan and the Nightmare*. Irving, TX: Spring Publications, Inc., 1979.

Holy Bible: Saint Joseph Textbook Edition. New York: Catholic Book Publishing Company, 1963.

Howell, Alice O. *Jungian Symbolism in Astrology*. Wheaton, IL: Quest Books, 1987.

_____. *Jungian Synchronicity in Astrological Signs and Ages*. Wheaton, IL: Quest Books, 1990.

Jacobi, Jolande. *Complex/Archetype/Symbol in the Psychology of C. G. Jung*. New York: Bollingen Paperback Edition, 1974.

_____. *The Psychology of C. G. Jung*. New Haven, CT: Yale University Press, 1973.

Jennings, Gary. *The Killer Storms: Hurricanes, Typhoons and Tornadoes.* New York: J. B. Lippincott Co., 1970.

Jung, C. G. *Analytical Psychology: Its Theory and Practice*. New York: Vintage Books, 1970.

_____. *C.G. Jung Speaking* (Bollingen Series XCVII). Ed. Wm. McGuire and R.F.C. Hull. Princeton: Princeton University Press, 1977.

_____. *The Collected Works* (Bollingen Series XX). 20 vols. Trans. R.F.C. Hull. Ed. H. Read, M. Fordham, G. Adler, Wm. McGuire. Princeton: Princeton University Press, 1953-1979.

_____. *Man and His Symbols*. New York: Doubleday and Company, Inc., 1964.

Larousse World Mythology. Ed. Pierre Grimal. New York: Excaliber Books, 1981.

Lee, Sally. *Hurricanes*. New York: Franklin Watts, 1993.

Mattoon, Mary Ann. *Understanding Dreams*. Dallas, TX: Spring Publications, 1984.

New Larousse Encyclopedia of Mythology. New York: The Hamlyn Publishing Group, 1983.

Neumann, Erich. *The Great Mother: An Analysis of the Archetype* (Bollingen Series XLVII). Princeton: Princeton University Press, 1991.

_____. *The Origins and History of Consciousness* (Bollingen Series XLII). Princeton: Princeton University Press, 1973.

Newton, David E. *Earthquakes*. New York: Franklin Watts, 1993.

Otto, Rudolf. *The Idea of the Holy*. New York: Oxford University Press, 1958.

Perera, Sylvia Brinton. *Descent to the Goddess: A Way of Initiation for Women*. Toronto: Inner City Books, 1981.

Powers, Jessica. *Selected Poetry of Jessica Powers*. Kansas City, MO: Sheed and Ward, 1989.

Poynter, Margaret. *Earthquakes: Looking for Answers*. Hillsdale, NJ: Enslow Publishers, Inc., 1990.

Rogets International Thesaurus. New York: Thomas Y. Crowell, 1979.

Saint Andrew Daily Missal, 1956. Bruges, Belgium: Desclée Debrouwner and Co., 1956.

Shakespeare, William. *The Complete Works*. London: Abbey Library, 1977.

Sharp, Daryl. *Jung Lexicon: A Primer of Terms and Concepts*. Toronto: Inner City Books, 1991.

Simon, Seymour. *Storms!!* New York: Morrow Junior Books, 1989.

Steele, Philip. *Weather Watch: Storms, Causes and Effects*. New York: Franklin Watts, 1991.

Twist, Clint. *Repairing the Damage: Hurricanes and Storms*. New York: Dillon Press, 1992.

Veninga, James F., and Wilmer, Harry A. *Vietnam in Remission*. College Station, TX: Texas A & M University Press, 1985.

Von Franz, Marie Louise. *C.G. Jung: His Myth in Our Time*. Trans. William H. Kennedy. New York: C.G. Jung Foundation, 1975.

_____. *An Introduction to the Psychology of Fairy Tales*. Irving, TX: Spring Publications, 1978.

Waite, A.E., trans. *The Hermetic and Alchemical Writings of Paracelsus*. New Hyde Park, NY: University Books, 1967.

Webster's New Universal Unabridged Dictionary. New York: New World Dictionaries/Simon and Schuster, 1983.

Whitmont, Edward C. *The Symbolic Quest: Basic Concepts of Analytical Psychology.* Princeton: Princeton University Press, 1978.

Wilhelm, Richard. *The I Ching or Book of Changes* (Bollingen Series XIX). Trans. Richard Wilhelm, rendered into English by Cary F. Baynes. Princeton: Princeton University Press, 1967.

Wilmer, Harry A. *Dreams of Vietnam.* New York: Free Press, 1985.

Woodman, Marion. *Addiction to Perfection: The Still Unravished Bride.* Toronto: Inner City Books, 1982.

_____. *The Pregnant Virgin: A Process of Psychological Transformation.* Toronto: Inner City Books, 1985.

Wright, Barton. *Hopi Kachinas.* Singapore: Northland Publishing, 1992.

Periodicals

National Geographic. National Geographic Society, Washington, DC., vol. 158, no. 3 (Sept. 1980).

Omni. Omni Publications International Ltd., New York, vol. 16, no. 6 (Mar. 1994).

Parabola: The Magazine of Myth & Tradition. "Power and Energy," in vol. 17, no. 4 (Nov. 1992).

Weatherwise. Helen Dwight Reid Educational Foundation, American Meteorological Society, Washington, DC., Dec. 1992-Jan. 1993.

Newspapers

St. Tammany News-Banner. Covington, LA. Sept. 9, 1992.

The Times-Picayune. New Orleans, LA. Aug. 25, 1992; Nov. 29, 1992; Jan. 5, 1993; Jan. 10, 1993; Feb. 7, 1993; Aug. 22, 1993; Sept. 19, 1993; Sept. 26, 1993; Nov. 7, 1993; April 26, 1994; Aug. 17, 1994.

Interviews

Breath, Rita. Survivor of Hurricane Camille (1969). Nov. 14, 1993.

Copes, Walter. Meteorologist with U. S. Weather Service. Slidell, LA. Oct. 5, 1993.

DesJardins, Peter. Witness to Hurricane Audrey (1957). Oct. 29-30, 1993.

Roberts, Jr., Nash. Meteorologist and hurricane forecaster in New Orleans. Jan. 24, 1994.

Thesis

Sedgwick, David. "The Psychology of the Counter-Transference: Transformative Aspects of the Analyst's Inner Process." Inter-Regional Society of Jungian Analysts, 1991.

Index

Page numbers in *italics* refer to illustrations

123

Studies in Jungian Psychology
by Jungian Analysts

Quality Paperbacks